# Contents

|  | Page |
|---|---|
| To the student | 5 |
| William Shakespeare | 7 |
| Understanding *A Midsummer Night's Dream*<br>(An exploration of the major topics and themes in the play.) | 12 |
| Analysis chart<br>(This shows important events, where they happen, time sequence, characters, and where to find them in the text and in this guide.) | 16 |
| Finding your way around the commentary | 18 |
| Commentary | 21 |
| Characters in the play | 57 |
| What happens in each act | 65 |
| Coursework and preparing for the examination | 71 |
|    Studying the text | 71 |
|    Writing the essay | 72 |
|    Sitting the examination | 74 |
| Glossary of literary terms | 77 |

# To the student

This study companion to your English literature text acts as a guide to the novel or play being studied. It suggests ways in which you can explore content and context, and focusses your attention on those matters which will lead to an understanding of, and an appreciative and sensitive response to the work of literature being studied.

Whilst this guide covers all those aspects dealt with in the traditional-style study aid, it is, more importantly, a flexible companion to study, enabling you to organize the patterns of study and priorities which reflect your particular needs at any given moment.

Whilst in many places descriptive, it is never prescriptive, always encouraging a sensitive personal response to a work of literature, rather than the shallow repetition of others' opinions. Such objectives have always been those of the good teacher, and have always assisted the student to gain high grades in GCSE examinations in English literature. These same factors are also relevant to students who are doing coursework in English literature for the purposes of continuous assessment.

The major part of this guide is the 'Commentary' where you will find a detailed commentary and analysis of all the important things you should know and study for your examination. There is also a section giving practical help on how to study a set text, write the type of essay that will gain high marks, prepare coursework and a guide to sitting examinations.

Used sensibly, this guide will be invaluable in your studies and help ensure your success in the course.

# William Shakespeare

Not much is known for certain about Shakespeare's private life but it matters little for an enjoyment of his plays. We know that he was born in 1564 and brought up in Stratford-on-Avon, that he went to London in 1586, wrote poetry, acted in the theatre and was co-author of some plays. He seems to have started writing plays under his own name in about 1591. He was a prolific writer, and within two or three years he produced several comedies and histories, as well as a sort of horror tragedy. Compared with the work of previous playwrights these early plays were outstanding for their style and characterization, but for Shakespeare they were merely an apprenticeship for his later work. He died in 1616.

## The sources of the plot

'. . . the most insipid ridiculous play that ever I saw in my life.'
Samuel Pepys (writing in 1662)

'. . . Shakespeare's best comedy.' Frank Kermode

Most critics agree that *A Midsummer Night's Dream* was probably written between 1595 and 1596, probably for performance at an aristocratic wedding celebration, although nobody seems sure which particular wedding it might have been. But it is clear that if the play was indeed written for a private wedding, Shakespeare at the same time had in mind the playhouse's regular, paying, audiences and wrote to please them also.

The society of rural Elizabethan England is probably the main source for the material in the play, being rich in legends of fairies, spirits, ghosts and supernatural creatures. Shakespeare's fairies, Puck, and even the more exotic Oberon and Titania are manifestations of the folklore which permeated Elizabethan society at this time. Although Shakespeare often used well-known figures as characters in his plays, he also usually relied on well-known contemporary stories and legends for his plots. *A Midsummer Night's Dream* seems to be an example of one of those relatively rare cases where he invented his own story.

## Structure of play

*A Midsummer Night's Dream* has an unusual structure. The play revolves around four different groups of characters and plots which are all allocated equal dramatic weights. Normally Shakespeare uses one or more sub-plots to run alongside or underneath the main action of his plays and it is usually fairly easy to tell which is a 'main' and which is a 'sub' plot. Sometimes his plays do not have any sub-plots, but here we have the unusual situation where a play is made up completely of four 'main' (or four 'sub') plots, each one featuring different kinds of characters and different kinds of dramatic action. These are skilfully woven together to form one whole, related structure and Shakespeare takes full advantage of the possibilities this provides for letting each plot link up with the others in various, effective ways. The four sub-plots from which the overall effect of the play is woven are:

1 The wedding of Theseus and Hippolyta

2 The love-tangles of Lysander, Demetrius, Hermia and Helena

3 The quarrel between Oberon and Titania

4 The Athenian workmen's rehearsal and performance of their play, *Pyramus and Thisbe*

These strands move the action of the play between different symbolic 'states'. The play begins in Athens during daylight. This symbolizes the state of being awake, of thinking clearly and of applying common sense and reason to the world. Next, the play moves into the twilight and darkness of a wood near Athens, which symbolizes a state of dreaming and unreality. Within the wood the influence of the bizarre and the irrational are triumphant. Finally, the play moves back into the daylight world of rationality. Although Theseus mentions a period of four days and nights, the play actually runs through only three clearly identifiable days and nights, although this technical inconsistency disappears during performances.

*A Midsummer Night's Dream* contains many visual contrasts, for example between the roughly dressed Athenian workmen and the courtly splendour of Theseus and Hippolyta, or between the braying, ass-headed Bottom and the sweetness and delicacy of Titania's fairy world. Such contrasts are also perceivable when you examine different characters, different moods and the different uses to which language is put–from the most beautiful poetry to the commonest prose. The extensive use which Shakespeare makes of rhyme in this play is a characteristic of his earlier work and here it is used mostly to create a dream-like atmosphere, or to mark off the everyday world from the world of fantasy.

This mixture of different elements permits the play to move in subtle ways between being funny and serious, rational and irrational. At times the action is an intriguing mixture of several elements at once. Often in the story, situations arise which look as though they will become tragic, but their dramatic treatment makes them less upsetting and reduces our anxiety. Humour is frequently used in this way: it is a kind of safety valve for rising emotions, as in Bottom's love scene with Titania. The workmen's portrayal of *Pyramus and Thisbe* is another example of a tragic theme which, because of its treatment, allows us to laugh at its ridiculous aspect. The overall effect of this continuous mixing and remixing of different dramatic elements is to reduce the emphasis on individual characters or individual stories and transfer it to an all-pervading atmosphere or mood which the play generates. This atmosphere is itself generated out of the mixture of the different elements within the drama.

The characteristic atmosphere of the play is that of a dream. Because a play is itself a sort of dream, in that what we are watching in a theatre is not 'real', this is a powerful dramatic device and Shakespeare uses it to encourage the audience to consider what we mean by 'reality'. Just as with actual dreams, the play seems plausible and real enough at the time, but afterwards we might wonder which is more meaningful or true, the world of dreams or the world of reality. In Elizabethan times Midsummer night itself was thought to be a magical time during which young women might be granted a glimpse of the future and see their prospective husbands. It was thought to be a time when the forces of the imagination held greater sway than those of logic, when extraordinary things were commonplace under the mysterious illumination of the moonlight.

*'Setting the scene'*

Oberon: *'Ill met by moonlight, proud Titania!'*

Helena: *'Nor does this wood lack worlds of company . . .'*

Titania: *'Sleep thou, and I will wind thee in my arms.'*

Theseus: *'If we imagine no worse of them than they of themselves, they may pass for excellent men.'*

# Understanding A Midsummer Night's Dream
## An exploration of the major topics and themes in the play

*Summaries of themes*

### Darkness

The world of darkness is used as the setting for much of the fairies' magic in the play. We are also encouraged to recognize that 'darkness', in the sense of being unable to understand (being 'in the dark' about something) is also common. In this context it is interesting to note that Shakespeare mentions 'eyes' in *A Midsummer Night's Dream* far more often than he does in any of his other plays.

The actual darkness of the woods is a parallel for the emotional and intellectual muddle in which many of the characters find themselves. We find that some characters become confused about their feelings for each other because whenever they meet they seem to have changed. The distinction between what is real and what *seems* real is a problem for many characters in the play. In this way many of them are 'in the dark' in several senses.

### Discord

The powerful storm which breaks out in nature because Oberon and Titania have become estranged is only one of the ways in which the play illustrates the destructiveness of discord. The suggestion is that it is equally damaging, although perhaps not quite so visible, in the world of humans also. Discord is equated with things which are unnatural, from the weather to beasts and nightmares. The play charts a variety of actions and characters who travel from discord to harmony, or order. This was a favourite theme of both Shakespeare and Elizabethan art generally. There are many contrasts within the play which are used to illustrate the theme of discord, some of which are discussed in detail in the commentary, although you should be alert for other instances.

### Illusion

The imagination is so powerful that it can create terrifying illusions, as the lovers and Bottom discover. Illusions can be more convincing than reality. The play uses this to question the nature of what is 'real' to us. A good example of this is the confusion in the minds of the four young lovers when they awaken from their sleep during Act Five.

Sleep is a time when the boundaries between the world of reality and the world of the irrational are blurred and this is exploited by Shakespeare, who uses this to show how the illusions created within sleep are in many ways just as real as those which inhabit everyday life.

There are several occasions when characters sleep in *A Midsummer Night's Dream*. Titania sleeps in the second scene of Act One when Oberon puts the love juice on her eyes. Puck anoints Lysander's eyes when he and Hermia sleep and Puck gets him confused with Demetrius. Demetrius falls asleep in the second scene of Act Three, when he becomes exhausted after failing to catch Hermia. This is when the love juice is put on his eyes. At the end of that second scene all four of the young lovers are made to fall asleep and it is during this period that the antidote to the love potion is put on Lysander's eyes. The same treatment that is given to Lysander is given also to Titania when she sleeps in the first scene in Act Four. Finally, and appropriately, Bottom sleeps at the end of the first scene in Act Four–appropriate, because when he awakens we begin to understand that the whole play is in some senses 'Bottom's Dream'. This becomes clearer when we look at how he describes his experience.

All together there are ten occasions when seven different characters sleep on stage–and three of them fall asleep twice.

## Imagination

At the end of the play we find Theseus and Puck emphasizing the importance of imagination. Theseus tells Hippolyta that imagination is needed by the audience if the actors' work is to be successful, and Puck reminds the audience that the play as a whole is only given substance through the imagination of the watchers. We also see an amusing example of what happens when imagination is inadequately applied, in the workmen's performance of *Pyramus and Thisbe*. It is also worth looking carefully at Theseus's speech at the start of Act Five, for it is the most powerful explanation of how essential–and dangerous–the human imagination is, especially if it is allowed to become too powerful. Like the rest of the play, Theseus's speech argues for humans to maintain a balance between passion and thought.

## Love

The play encourages us to think about the difference between 'doting', which is the notion of being in love without the substance of it, and real love, which is more mature. The play suggests that mature love involves something more than just raw emotion–it involves reason also. Theseus and Hippolyta, for example, have a love which seems to be a mixture of passion and thoughtfulness. Marriage is portrayed as the proper outcome of true love, and the quarrel between Titania and Oberon is used to show how the whole of the world of nature is disturbed by any breaking up of their relationship. The implication is that true love leads to harmony in marriage, but leads to discord and chaos when lovers quarrel. This is echoed through the use of imagery which mentions Cupid and Diana. Cupid, the wingèd Roman god of love, is shown as blind, irrational and impetuous with his dangerous bow and arrows of love (discord) whilst Diana is associated with chastity and restraint (harmony).

## Moon

The moon exerts its influence throughout the play, mainly through the imagery. It is seen at the start of the play as a pent up force which is about to release its influence upon the world

> '. . . like to a silver bow
> New-bent in heaven . . .'

Time is measured by the moon for all characters in the play and her power over large parts of the world, like the tides, is stressed frequently. Shakespeare mentions the moon and moonlight more often in *A Midsummer Night's Dream* than in any other play he wrote. These frequent references emphasize the dream-world quality of the play, where the moon is depicted as cold and fruitless, but mysterious and powerful in its influence.

## Music

Music is used in the play, along with dancing or singing, as a symbol of happiness, harmony and order. Occasions when music is used increase noticeably towards the end of the play, as the drama moves from discord and chaos to harmony and order. Music is also mentioned frequently in the context of the fairies, which brings out its magical qualities. This links it with the theme of order.

## Mythology

There are many references to classical mythology in the play, which is not surprising when we recall its setting. The play is not *about* mythology but uses many mythological references which would have been well known to Shakespeare's audience. These references are used throughout the play to 'comment' on the characters and the action and, because they may be unfamiliar to some modern students, several important examples have been discussed in detail in the commentary. These references often tell us much about what is going on in the play at any given moment so it is worth noting the kind of associations which are being suggested. The context in which mythological references are used is important, and these references also underpin other themes in the play.

In Act One we find mention of Diana, the Roman goddess of chastity, the moon and hunting, who is also mentioned by her other name, Phoebe. We hear about Venus, the Roman goddess of love and Cupid. The Greek god of the sun, 'Phibbus' (Phoebus), is referred to along with Hercules (although Bottom, typically, calls him 'Ercles'). The sad love story of *Pyramus and Thisbe* is also mentioned. These are appropriate at the start of the play, when it is clear that love is an important theme and the passage of time will be referenced to the moon throughout.

In Act Two there are references to Corin and Phillida, who were two imaginary, traditional lovers. In keeping with the rising discord between the lovers, we find mention of several of Theseus's old flames from classical literature: Perigenia, Aegles, and Ariadne. Neptune, the god of the sea is mentioned as is the god of light, Apollo, who was also the god of music and poetry. These references are used to identify certain characters as having something in common with the forces of nature or the power of music and dancing; connections are being suggested with the themes of discord and harmony.

In Act Three we find Ninus mentioned, who was the builder of Babylon, where Pyramus and Thisbe lived. Venus is mentioned again, and the imagery of light and the moon is developed to include dawn with the mention of Aurora, the goddess of the rising sun.

In Act Four Diana is mentioned again, and another reference to ancient Athens occurs when Theseus talks about how his dogs come from Sparta, which was a city state near ancient Greece. Another connection with animals and classical Greece is made when bulls of Thessalian origin are mentioned. Thessaly was a large division of ancient Greece.

In Act Five several references to ancient Greece occur, with references to centaurs (half horse, half man), Thebes (an ancient Greek city) and Bacchus (the Greek god of wine). The nine sister goddesses known as the Muses are mentioned, as is a famous Greek lover, Leander (or 'Limander', as Bottom calls him). The Furies are spoken about also–they were daughters of Night, and were responsible for wreaking vengeance on the part of the other gods. The Fates are an appropriate group of goddesses to find in the play, for they controlled the destiny of men. Hecate, the ruler of Hell and Heaven as well as earth, is also mentioned in the play as a force in nature with power over the lives of humans.

## Nature

The world of nature is seen to be populated with all manner of insects, animals and forces, from delicate flowers to the 'dragons of the night'. Many of these are referred to in the play and some are discussed in the commentary. Look out for all such examples, to see if you can work out why they have been used on such occasions and why they are appropriate: for example, bats were not well regarded because it was thought that witches sometimes travelled disguised as them; crows were also considered to be a bad omen; butterflies might be the souls of the dead; and spiders meant good luck.

The fairies themselves are, of course, the most powerful expression of the forces hidden within the natural world, and we see how closely they are identified with it on many occasions. The most beautiful and evocative connection between the fairies and their natural world occurs in Act Two, where Titania's bower is described. The power of Oberon's love juice is also seen as something distilled from nature and this emphasizes the mysterious powers which are hidden within the natural world. The moon, as part of the world of nature, is another mysterious and ambiguous force which exerts its influence throughout the play.

You should notice also the way the world of nature is depicted as vibrant and bursting with life and activity, even when to humans it seems silent – such as at night. One aspect of the imagery which reveals this is the use made of colour. At one extreme the moon seems pale and barren and its light seems to bleach life from everything. At the opposite extreme the dawn sunrise is watched by Oberon:

> 'Even till the eastern gate all fiery red
> Opening on Neptune with fair blessèd beams
> Turns into yellow gold his salt green streams.' (III.2)

Colours are mentioned often in the play in the context of birds, flowers, fruit and the eyes and lips of young women. It is worth looking for examples to see how beautifully Shakespeare uses them.

## Order

The play travels from discord through to order. Order was thought of in Elizabethan times as an important characteristic of all things, both in the natural and man-made worlds. Without order chaos would reign. It was therefore important that people respected and upheld all forms of order and authority. The Elizabethans saw order throughout the world of nature and this is a strong theme in *A Midsummer Night's Dream*. At the opening of the play we see how Theseus has to deal with a father whose daughter is rebelling against his authority. The ordered relationship between Oberon and Titania is under threat. The four young lovers eventually arrive at a harmonious and ordered state, but only after we have seen how potentially destructive disorder can be. The destructive power of disorder is demonstrated in the human and fairy worlds, and a comical example of it is to be found in the workmen's struggles to perform *Pyramus and Thisbe*, something which they themselves appropriately describe as a 'most lamentable comedy'.

# Analysis chart

| | | Act One | | | | | | | | | Act |  |  |  |  |  |  |
|---|---|---|---|---|---|---|---|---|---|---|---|---|---|---|---|---|---|
| | Scene | 1 | | | | | | 2 | | | 1 | | | | | | |
| **Worlds:** | Human | ■ | ■ | ■ | ■ | ■ | ■ | | | | | ■ | ■ | | | | |
| | Workmen | | | | | | | | | ■ | | | | | | | |
| | Magical | | | | | | | | | | | ■ | ■ | ■ | ■ | ■ | ■ | ■ |
| **Important events** | | Theseus announces his marriage | Egeus comes to complain about Hermia | Theseus advises Hermia | Lysander and Hermia vow their love | Lysander and Hermia agree to run away | The problem of Demetrius | Lysander and Hermia tell Helena their plan | Helena decides to tell Demetrius the plan | The 'casting' of the workmen's play | Puck tells of the rift between Oberon and Titania | Oberon and Titania argue about the boy | Oberon decides to use the magic juice | Demetrius chases Hermia in the wood | Helena chases Demetrius in the wood | Oberon vows to help Hermia | Oberon visits Titania with the magic juice |
| **Themes:** | Darkness | | | | | | ● | | | | ● | | | | | | |
| | Discord | ● | ● | ● | | ● | ● | | | | ● | ● | ● | ● | ● | | |
| | Illusion | | ● | | | | | ● | ● | ● | ● | | | ● | | ● | |
| | Imagination | | | | | ● | | | | | | | ● | | ● | | ● |
| | Love | ● | ● | ● | ● | ● | ● | | ● | ● | | | | | ● | | |
| | Moon | ● | ● | ● | | | | ● | | ● | ● | ● | | | | ● | |
| | Music | | ● | | | | | | | | ● | | | | | | |
| | Mythology | ● | | | | | | | ● | ● | ● | | | ● | | | |
| | Nature | | | | | | | | | | ● | ● | ● | ● | ● | ● | ● |
| | Order | ● | ● | ● | | | | | | | | | | | | | |
| **Characters:** | Bottom | | | | | | | | | ● | | | ● | | | | |
| | Demetrius | | | | | | ● | | | | | | | ● | ● | | |
| | Egeus | ● | ● | ● | | | | | | | | | | | | ● | |
| | Helena | | | | | | ● | | ● | | | | | ● | ● | ● | |
| | Hermia | | ● | ● | ● | ● | | | | ● | | | | | | | |
| | Hippolyta | ● | | | | | | | | | | ● | | | | | |
| | Lysander | | | | ● | ● | | ● | | ● | | | | | | ● | |
| | Oberon | | | | | | | | | | ● | ● | ● | | | ● | ● |
| | Puck | | | | | | ● | | | | ● | | ● | | | ● | |
| | Quince | | | | | | | | | ● | | | | | | | |
| | Theseus | ● | ● | ● | | | | | | | ● | ● | | | | ● | |
| | Titania | | | | | | | | | | ● | ● | ● | | | | |
| | Workmen | | | | | | | | | ● | | | | | | | |
| | Comment no | 1 | 3 | 6 | 9 | 10 | 12 | 13 | 14 | 15 | 18 | 24 | 27 | 30 | 31 | 32 | 33 |

| | Two | | Act Three | | Act Four | | Act Five |
|---|---|---|---|---|---|---|---|
| | 2 | | 1 | 2 | 1 | 2 | 1 |

| Love juice is put on Titania's eyes | Hermia and Lysander fall asleep in the wood | Puck puts love juice on Lysander's eyes | Lysander awakens and falls in love with Helena | Hermia awakens from a nightmare. Lysander is gone | The rehearsal of the workmen's play | Bottom becomes an ass | Titania falls in love with Bottom | Puck reports to Oberon | Oberon puts love juice on Demetrius's eyes. Demetrius falls in love with Helena | Helena and Hermia fall out | Puck separates and exhausts the lovers – who sleep | Titania falls asleep with Bottom | Oberon releases Titania from the charm | Theseus and Egeus hear Lysander's story | The lovers discuss their experiences in the wood | Bottom awakens from his dream | The workmen make ready to perform their play | Theseus and Hippolyta discuss the lovers' stories | The workmen's play is introduced | The workmen's play is performed | The humans depart to bed | The fairies come to guard the humans | Puck addresses the theatre audience |
|---|---|---|---|---|---|---|---|---|---|---|---|---|---|---|---|---|---|---|---|---|---|---|---|
| 34 | 35 | 36 | 37 | 40 | 41 | 45 | 48 | 50 | 51 | 52 | 55 | 59 | 61 | 63 | 66 | 68 | 69 | 70 | 72 | 75 | 81 | 84 | 86 |

# Finding your way around the commentary

**Each page of the commentary gives the following information:**

1. A quotation from the start of each paragraph on which a comment is made, or act/scene or line numbers plus a quotation, so that you can easily locate the right place in your text.

2. A series of comments, explaining, interpreting, and drawing your attention to important incidents, characters and aspects of the text.

3. For each comment, headings to indicate the important characters, themes, and ideas dealt with in the comment.

4. For each heading, a note of the comment numbers in this guide where the previous or next comment dealing with that heading occurred.

**Thus you can use this commentary section in a number of ways.**

1. Turn to that part of the commentary dealing with the chapter/act you are perhaps revising for a class discussion or essay. Read through the comments in sequence, referring all the time to the text, which you should have open before you. The comments will direct your attention to all the important things of which you should take note.

2. Take a single character or topic from the list on page 19. Note the comment number next to it. Turn to that comment in this guide, where you will find the first of a number of comments on your chosen topic. Study it, and the appropriate part of your text to which it will direct you. Note the comment number in this guide where the next comment for your topic occurs and turn to it when you are ready. Thus, you can follow one topic right through your text. If you have an essay to write on a particular character or theme just follow the path through this guide and you will soon find everything you need to know!

3. A list of relevant relationships between certain topics will be found on page 19. To find these in the guide turn to the comment indicated. As the previous and next comment are printed at the side of each page in the commentary, it is a simple matter to flick through the pages to find the previous or next occurrence of the relationship in which you are interested.

For example, you want to examine in depth the character of Demetrius. Turning to the character list, you will find that he is first discussed in comment 12. On turning to comment 12 you will discover a zero (0) in the place of the previous reference (because this is the first time that he has been discussed) and the number 30 for the next reference. You now turn to comment 30 and find that the previous comment number is 12 (from where you have just been looking) and that the next reference is to comment 31, and so on throughout the text.

You also wish to trace the relationship between discord and Bottom throughout the play. From the relationships list, you are directed to comment 27. This is the first time that both discord and Bottom are discussed together. You will now discover that two different comment numbers are given for the subject under examination – numbers 30 and 41. This is because each topic is considered separately as well as together and you will have to continue tracing them separately until you come to comment 42 – the next occasion on which both discord and Bottom are discussed.

Finding your way around the commentary

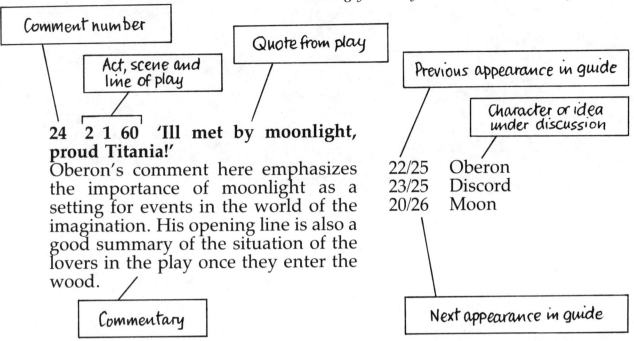

## Single topics:

| | Comment no: | | Comment no: |
|---|---|---|---|
| Darkness | 10 | Bottom | 16 |
| Discord | 2 | Demetrius | 12 |
| Illusion | 3 | Egeus | 1 |
| Imagination | 10 | Helena | 12 |
| Love | 1 | Hermia | 6 |
| Moon | 1 | Hippolyta | 1 |
| Music | 3 | Lysander | 8 |
| Mythology | 1 | Oberon | 20 |
| Nature | 18 | Puck | 13 |
| Order | 1 | Quince | 15 |
| | | Theseus | 1 |
| | | Titania | 19 |
| | | Workmen | 16 |

## Relationships:

| | | | Comment no: | | | | Comment no: |
|---|---|---|---|---|---|---|---|
| Discord | and | Bottom | 27 | Nature | and | Oberon | 22 |
| | and | Egeus | 3 | | and | Puck | 18 |
| | and | Helena | 12 | | and | Titania | 19 |
| | and | Lysander | 8 | | and | Imagination | 26 |
| | and | Puck | 21 | | | | |
| | and | Workmen | 42 | Illusion | and | Puck | 13 |
| | and | Music | 3 | | and | Moon | 3 |
| | | | | | and | Love | 14 |
| Love | and | Demetrius | 12 | Order | and | Theseus | 1 |
| | and | Hermia | 6 | | and | Music | 62 |
| | and | Lysander | 9 | | | | |
| | and | Oberon | 55 | | | | |
| | and | Theseus | 1 | | | | |

# Commentary

'. . . the moon—like to a silver bow
New bent in heaven . . .'

# Act 1, scene 1

**1   1 1 1   'Now, fair Hippolyta, ...'**

This first scene introduces several important themes in the play. Different forms of authority are represented by the figures of Theseus and Egeus. Mature love is shown as being passionate but steady and restrained – capable of waiting and culminating in marriage. Young love is shown as being powerful and fickle – the young lovers will change and rechange their allegiances during the play. Love it seems, even in the spirit world, is not without its problems and causes both great joy and great anguish until its passions are resolved. It is in the wood that these passions will be worked out.

Theseus and Hippolyta are impatient for their wedding to take place, and we see this contrast between their impatience and the slow dragging of time in the way the language is used. For example, notice the effect of phrases such as 'how slow this old moon wanes' and the use of words like 'lingers' and 'withering' to suggest suffering and the slow passage of time.

The opening of the play is very lyrical and sets the romantic tone for this comedy of love. We can see straight away that marriage is regarded as something very important, noble and wonderful. As such this is no time for feeling depressed and that is why Theseus tells Philostrate to go and 'turn melancholy forth'.

The importance of the moon as an image in the play is emphasized right at the start – it is mentioned directly three times in the first ten lines of the play and over thirty times by its end. There are also several mentions of the huntress Diana, the Roman goddess of the moon and of chastity. Diana's bow, like Cupid's, will soon be 'new-bent in heaven' according to Hippolyta. The imagery of the moon in the play is therefore not only a marker of time and a bringer of romance, it is also symbolic of the influence of dreams and the power of the imagination and the unreal over the lives of people. This opening scene in the play is the only one which occurs in daylight.

*Characters and ideas previous/next comment*

| | |
|---|---|
| 0/3 | Egeus |
| 0/25 | Hippolyta |
| 0/2 | Theseus |
| 0/2 | Love |
| 0/3 | Moon |
| 0/13 | Mythology |
| 0/5 | Order |

---

**2   1 1 12   'Stir up the Athenian youth ...'**

In this speech Theseus gives us important information about the relationship between himself and Hippolyta:

> '... I wooed thee with my sword,
> And won thy love doing thee injuries;'

Each relationship that we see in the play begins, when we first meet the characters, with a state of conflict, chaos or discord. Theseus first meets Hippolyta in battle; Egeus enters the action in fury at his daughter Hermia's disobedience; Lysander and Hermia are lovers forced apart; Helena's love for Demetrius is not returned by him; the workmen's arrangements for their play are chaotic; and Puck tells us that jealous Oberon is 'passing fell and wrath' because Titania has taken the young boy for herself.

All of these conflicts are resolved harmoniously by the end of the play. Theseus's comment about winning someone's love by 'doing them injuries' applies to all these relationships in one way or another. *A Midsummer Night's Dream* stresses that discord can always be resolved into harmony and Oberon, who plays the part of a kindly providence, is an important agent in ensuring that harmony prevails in the end. Notice, however, that all of these discordant relationships are resolved only through some kind of suffering. Shakespeare seems to be suggesting that love, by its very nature, leaves people at risk from conflict and discord.

| | |
|---|---|
| 1/3 | Theseus |
| 0/3 | Discord |
| 1/4 | Love |

---

**3   1 1 22   'Full of vexation come I, ...'**

Although Theseus has just said that this is no time for melancholy, it looks as though it has appeared, nevertheless, with the entrance of Egeus and his complaint. The play is full of this kind of contrast of mood and, as we notice when we compare Egeus with Theseus, of character and temperament.

| | |
|---|---|
| 1/4 | Egeus |
| 2/4 | Theseus |
| 2/4 | Discord |
| 0/13 | Illusion |

*Act 1* 23

*Characters and ideas*
*previous/next comment*

In contrast to Theseus's public and very proper wooing of Hippolyta after their battle, Egeus complains that his daughter Hermia has been 'bewitched' by Lysander and now wants to marry him, instead of Demetrius who already had Egeus's consent. Notice, when you read the lines which Egeus speaks, the references to moonlight, dreams, songs, cunning, trifles and other kinds of 'feigning' (pretending). The importance of the dream/reality contrasts in the play are therefore emphasized right at its beginning.

| 1/6 | Moon |
| 0/4 | Music |

Notice also the cleverly built-in stage directions. Egeus calls Demetrius and Lysander out in turn, supposedly to show Theseus who they are, but also to introduce them to the audience. How far would you agree that it is the case that Egeus prefers Demetrius to Lysander because of prejudice rather than as a result of any logical considerations?

### 4  1 1 30  'Thou hast by moonlight . . .'

Egeus accuses Lysander of 'filching' his daughter's heart by the use of cunning. He has sung love songs under her window by moonlight, given her presents, written her poetry, exchanged locks of hair with her and thereby, says Egeus, 'bewitched' her.

| 3/5 | Egeus |
| 3/6 | Theseus |
| 3/6 | Discord |
| 2/6 | Love |
| 3/18 | Music |

The theme of the conflict between youth and age is one which appears in several of Shakespeare's plays and also in much other Elizabethan literature. Many of the things which Egeus says Lysander has been doing were traditionally associated with lovers. You will probably recognize many of them as still being part of the behaviour of lovers today. Theseus is older than Lysander and Hermia, but younger than Egeus, and is in love himself. As a wise head of state, Theseus supports Egeus in principle but modifies the letter of the law to suit circumstances later on.

### 5  1 1 42  'As she is mine . . .'

Today we may find Egeus's attitude towards his daughter rather extreme; he refers to her as something he owns. We might also think it rather foolish of him to demand the death penalty for Lysander. However, in Elizabethan times the authority of a father was much stronger and more respected and Theseus's remarks about how Egeus should be like 'a god' to Hermia would not have seemed out of place. Many of Shakespeare's audience would probably have thought that Egeus's anger at his daughter's disobedience was well founded. It would have been understood by the audience that, here, Egeus is being used as the 'stock' figure of Age, imposing its sterile will upon the passions of Youth.

| 4/6 | Egeus |
| 1/6 | Order |

### 6  1 1 46  'What say you, Hermia? . . .'

The conversation which starts here between Hermia and Theseus shows the audience how a wise and mature ruler like Theseus deals with complaints like this one by Egeus. Theseus is the ruler of Athens and it is his job to see that the laws are obeyed. On the other hand, as someone in love himself, he probably feels compassion for the young woman in front of him. His wisdom is shown when he suggests that she examine her feelings carefully, and when he postpones his decision until the next new moon, which is the day of his own wedding.

| 5/8 | Egeus |
| 0/7 | Hermia |
| 4/7 | Theseus |
| 4/8 | Discord |
| 4/7 | Love |
| 3/7 | Moon |
| 5/50 | Order |

There is a very real conflict here – the right of a woman to marry the man she loves versus the right of a father to guide his daughter's behaviour. If the law has its way the woman could face death, and if she obeys her father she faces the possibility of a life bound to a man she no longer loves. This incident contributes to one of the traditional features of the play by introducing a deliberate twist to the plot which threatens the happiness of the two young lovers. It is an incident which also heightens dramatic tension.

Given the situation and bearing in mind the rules which Theseus must be seen to be obeying himself, what would you have advised Hermia to do? See also if

## Act 1

you can understand why Egeus behaves as he does. His attitude, although harsh, is not really unreasonable given the kind of society he lives in. You should also bear in mind that in this play many of the characters are used as 'types' by Shakespeare, so here we have Theseus the 'wise ruler' and Egeus the authoritarian 'angry father'. The lovers and the workmen are treated in the same way; more information on this can be found in the section on 'Characters in the Play' which begins on page 57.

---

### 7   1 1 65   'Either to die the death, . . .'

Theseus explains to Hermia that enforced chastity is as sterile as 'the cold fruitless moon'. He also suggests that the state of imposed virginity is unnatural by the use of words like 'endure', 'mewed' (cooped up like poultry or hawks), and 'barren'. This is countered by Hermia with the arguments that she will never agree to give her virginity to someone unless her 'soul consents'. As you read this speech by Hermia, notice the careful use of the word 'sovereignty'. Queen Elizabeth I was famous as 'the virgin Queen' and Hermia, as a character in a play by Shakespeare, is praising the nobility of those who freely decide to remain virgins. Such royal flattery was a commonplace in Elizabethan art and a careful reading of *A Midsummer Night's Dream* will unearth several other examples of it. Shakespeare is also using Hermia as an example of 'the disobedient daughter', about which the Elizabethans had strong views – parents expected respect and obedience from children, not wilfulness and argument.

| | |
|---|---|
| 6/ 9 | Hermia |
| 6/ 8 | Theseus |
| 6/ 9 | Love |
| 6/ 13 | Moon |

---

### 8   1 1 111   'I must confess that . . .'

In this speech we get a hint that Theseus does not altogether agree with Egeus and Demetrius, which may be why he takes them off for some 'private schooling'. The world 'schooling' here can mean both 'instruction' and 'disciplining' and it is a neat ambiguity as to whether Theseus is going to give them advice on how to get their way or whether he is going to tell them off. In either case, it is clear that Theseus recognizes, as we should, that there are two sides to this dispute, each with a measure of right. What do you imagine Theseus actually says to the two men? Do you think he intends to speak his mind, or will he try to be as tactful as he can? What, if you were Theseus, would you think of Hermia, Lysander and Demetrius at this point in the play? Consider what Lysander, who has not yet spoken, might be thinking of Egeus at this point.

| | |
|---|---|
| 6/ 32 | Egeus |
| 0/ 9 | Lysander |
| 7/ 20 | Theseus |
| 6/ 10 | Discord |

---

### 9   1 1 128   'How now my love? . . .'

This famous duet between Lysander and Hermia explores the many difficulties which love struggles to overcome and contains the famous observation by Lysander that 'the course of true love never did run smooth'. This is an important dramatic point in Shakespeare's play.

| | |
|---|---|
| 7/ 11 | Hermia |
| 8/ 10 | Lysander |
| 7/ 11 | Love |

The rest of this scene is quite sad, and may, if you have read it, remind you in its general tone of *Romeo and Juliet*, which was written at about the same time in Shakespeare's career as *A Midsummer Night's Dream*.

---

### 10   1 1 156   'A good persuasion. . . .'

In this speech Lysander arranges that he and Hermia will meet in the wood outside Athens the following night. This is the wood which will have such a large part to play in *A Midsummer Night's Dream*. All the main characters in the play gather in this wood, and it acts as both a place of darkness and danger, and a place of mystery, magic and unreality. It is in the wood that the lovers' feelings will be put to the test. It is in the wood that the worlds of the impossible and the real collide, blur and transform one into the other. It is interesting to note that, for the Elizabethans, a common alternative meaning for the word 'wood' was 'mad'.

| | |
|---|---|
| 9/ 13 | Lysander |
| 0/ 20 | Darkness |
| 8/ 12 | Discord |
| 0/ 26 | Imagination |

*Characters and ideas previous/ next comment*

## Act 1

*Characters and ideas previous/next comment*

**11  1 1 169  'I swear to thee by Cupid's . . .'**
Hermia's speech marks a change in the use of language in this scene. From here to the end of it the verse is in rhymed couplets, whereas up until now it has not been. Shakespeare generally used poetry when noble characters spoke, or when the subject matter of conversation changed to noble issues. But here the effect of the repeated couplets is to produce a rather artificial and patterned feeling to what is said in rhymed couplets. We therefore tend not to take what the characters say too seriously. By this neat device Shakespeare contrasts what the lovers are saying to each other, which is rather sad and tragic, with the manner in which it is said, which is rather stilted and emotionally unconvincing. This helps to maintain the scene on its comic course. The rather artificial language also emphasizes the formal and courtly love which these two characters have for each other; this familiar theatrical device is one which Shakespeare's audience would have quickly recognized.

9/12  Hermia
9/12  Love

**12  1 1 198  'The more I hate, . . .'**
Hermia is referring to Demetrius when she says this. On the next line Helena uses the same pattern of words to reverse the meaning when she says 'The more I love, the more he hateth me'. This use of pattern and rhyming couplets has a similar effect as that we saw at line 169, which is that the *way* in which these women speak makes what they say sound less upsetting than what they seem to mean. This means that whilst we might be able to sympathize with Helena's plight we do not feel that her anguish is something we can get very upset about. The use of verse means that we simply cannot take her all that seriously from an emotional point of view, but we can hear and accept the dramatic argument from her. The other effect this device produces here is that by having them speak alternate lines it also emphasizes the sympathy which the two women have for each other.

0/30  Demetrius
0/14  Helena
11/16 Hermia
10/21 Discord
11/14 Love

**13  1 1 208  'Helen, to you our minds . . .'**
The play is full of references to moonlight, especially its mysterious qualities. Lysander talks here of Phoebe, the female goddess of the moon, as studying her night-time reflection in the oceans. The suggestion is that Phoebe is watchful during the night, when lovers run away together as Lysander and Hermia plan to do. Again we can see the link between the measuring and passage of time and the moon. Throughout the play there is a suggestion that the moon and moonlight have a mysterious power and influence over mankind, that the moon and its light both measure and to some extent control time and reality, which is something we see especially during the scenes in the wood. Another good example of this idea occurs in the speech Puck makes towards the end of the play:

10/16 Lysander
0/18  Puck
3/14  Illusion
7/17  Moon
1/14  Mythology

> 'And we fairies, that do run
> By the triple Hecate's team
> From the presence of the sun,
> Following darkness like a dream,
> Now are frolic . . .'

Puck is suggesting that whatever powers the fairies have, they are connected to moonlight not sunlight. The fairies belong, like the dreams which they follow, to the mysterious world of Phoebe. Throughout the play we find that the connection between moonlight and dreaming is very strong.

**14  1 1 226  'How happy some o'er other . . .'**
This starts the first soliloquy in the play. It is important that it is spoken by Helena, who is the female character who will suffer most before the end of the play. This speech maintains the ambiguous atmosphere of the scene, ensuring that it finishes on a sad but not too serious note.

12/27 Helena
13/15 Illusion
12/15 Love
13/15 Mythology

Helena, a few lines further on, talks about 'Things base and vile'. This part of her soliloquy states an important theme of the play about the way love can rob people of their judgement or common sense. By 'looking with the eyes' she means seeing things as they really are. By 'looking with the mind' she is referring to the way love can change, or 'transpose', crude and ugly things into objects of beauty and dignity. This is another example of the 'blind Cupid' idea which appears several times in the play and to which you should be alert. The interesting point to note is that Helena recognizes that love can therefore give to people qualities which they do not actually possess, yet at the same time she is unable to stop herself from loving Demetrius, who treats her terribly. A knowledge of the 'disease' of love evidently does not help with finding a cure.

We will see in the rest of the play that Helena is quite right in her observation; love often changes ordinary reality in a completely irrational way. Characters see the world through their imagination not through their eyes. Knowledge that this may be happening makes no difference to the effect being produced on a character and does not make them immune from love's influences.

## Scene 2

**15   1 2 11   'Marry, our play is . . .'**
Quince tells the assembled workmen that their play will be *Pyramus and Thisbe*. This famous classical story of thwarted love would have been well known to Shakespeare's audience. Notice how this theme has already been introduced into the main play in the first scene. This kind of dramatic 'echo' of one story set against another is used frequently in Shakespeare's play and it enables him to let one story play against the other in an illuminating way.

| | |
|---|---|
| 0/17 | Quince |
| 14/17 | Illusion |
| 14/16 | Love |
| 14/27 | Mythology |

**16   1 2 22   'That will ask some tears . . .'**
Typically, Bottom is full of enthusiasm about playing the lover Pyramus, but feels that the role he would really like is that of a tyrant, although his demonstration of how he would do it is typically ham-fisted.

It is worth noting, as we smile at Bottom's puppy-like enthusiasm, that what he says contains more truth than appears on the surface, for the role of love in *A Midsummer Night's Dream* will indeed be that of a kind of tyrant – all powerful, irrational, and bewildering by turns as it adopts its many illusions and transformations.

| | |
|---|---|
| 0/27 | Bottom |
| 12/35 | Hermia |
| 13/32 | Lysander |
| 0/41 | Workmen |
| 15/31 | Love |

Notice also that, in keeping with the change of atmosphere between this scene and the one before it, the language switches from poetry back into prose. The humour of the scene comes largely from the way these unsophisticated workmen take themselves extremely seriously and show us, by the ludicrous and over enthusiastic 'ham' acting methods they suggest they will adopt, that the performance of a classical tragedy is quite beyond them. The title of their play is as strange as it is revealing, for *The Most Lamentable Comedy and Most Cruel Death of Pyramus and Thisbe* clearly mixes comedy and tragedy in a way which closely parallels the mixture in the previous scene and in Shakespeare's play as a whole. *Pyramus and Thisbe* therefore represents what might have happened to Hermia and Lysander if Egeus had successfully got his way and, like the happenings within the wood, it will be a tragedy turned into a farce by the ignorance of the actors.

**17   1 2 90   'Some of your French crowns . . .'**
In this speech Quince bids the company of workmen learn their lines by the following night, when they are to meet in the wood by moonlight. Again we see the wood playing a part in secret meetings and hopes for the future and the moon playing a part in the measuring and passage of time. Notice carefully that the wood, as illuminated by moonlight, is also the location for the creation of illusion, as in the workmen's play, and a 'rehearsal' ready for a finished product to emerge into the public world of humans, as in the adventures and discoveries of the four young lovers.

| | |
|---|---|
| 15/41 | Quince |
| 15/18 | Illusion |
| 13/20 | Moon |

# Act Two

Puck: '... upon thy eyes I throw
All the power this charm doth owe.'

## Act Two, scene 1

**18  2 1 1  'How now, spirit; . . .'**
The fairy sings the first of the play's five main songs. Notice the fairy's use of rhyme here. All the songs are written in rhyme, as are the ends of most scenes, which was the convention in Elizabethan drama. Can you think why the use of rhyme at the ends of scenes was such a useful feature? Think about how difficult it might otherwise have been for a dramatist to signal to the audience that an incident, or scene, was ending.

Shakespeare often criticized bad acting in his plays, and several parts of *A Midsummer Night's Dream* are a parody of contemporary drama, from the title of the workmen's play to some of the 'over the top' acting and language which he gives to them. Many of Shakespeare's audience would have instantly recognized such wit and it probably contributed quite a lot to their enjoyment of an already brilliant play. Especially funny, even today, is the rehearsal and performance of *Pyramus and Thisbe* itself because most people have sat through an excruciating production of a play at some time.

This consideration about how any play should be produced raises an extremely important point about *A Midsummer Night's Dream* concerning the fairies. Even though we are far from clear about the details of the Elizabethans' views about such things as witches, spirits and fairies, we know that they had a rather more willing tolerance of the idea that such things existed than is often the case today. If you were staging a contemporary version of the play consider how you would depict the fairies. Would they be Disney-like, dancing figures with gossamer wings, scattering fairy-dust wherever they went, like Tinkerbell in *Peter Pan*? Would you even have them as visible creatures? You would have to overcome the central problem of making the audience believe in them, rather than risk the audience dismissing them as ridiculous and old-fashioned nonsense. Do you think that the play would be more successful if filmed, bearing in mind the special-effects resources available today? There are no correct answers to any of these questions, but it is important that you decide *how* you would tackle directing the play – remember that the play really 'exists' only when it is performed. Whilst we might be able to ignore the 'problem' of the fairies when we read the play to ourselves, it becomes a major consideration when it is performed in a theatre.

Shakespeare relied almost exclusively on words to create the effects in his plays and the use of 'props' was fairly minimal. But during the early 20th century some theatres populated the play's woods with real trees, rabbits, deer, squirrels and hares – all in addition to lighting effects, music and dancing. Modern critics often regard this sort of thing as vulgar distortion of the original character of the play. Try to decide for yourself whether you agree with such critics.

*Characters and ideas previous/next comment*

| | |
|---|---|
| 13/20 | Puck |
| 17/30 | Illusion |
| 4/34 | Music |
| 0/19 | Nature |

**19  2 1 10  'The cowslips tall . . .'**
The fairy begins with the first of many references in the conversation to small things. This is another contrast – that of scale – which is introduced here, emphasized by the mention of dewdrops and cowslips. Notice the way the flowers are personified – this is typical of the imagery throughout the play, which has a wide range of natural references. Why do you think personification was used here, rather than a straightforward image? A good clue lies in the word 'pensioners', which was the name given to the members of Queen Elizabeth's bodyguard and who were chosen for their good looks, good breeding and height. Pensioners wore uniforms embroidered with jewels and gold lace. Apart from the obvious beauty of the image, consider how this fits in with the idea that Titania is a royal person, and also how this imagery would have been flattering to Queen Elizabeth.

| | |
|---|---|
| 0/22 | Titania |
| 18/22 | Nature |

**20  2 1 18  'The King doth keep . . .'**
Just as Act One opened in the court of Theseus, a mortal, in daylight, Act Two opens in the fairy court of Oberon in moonlight. This is emphasized by the

| | |
|---|---|
| 0/22 | Oberon |
| 18/21 | Puck |

number of times 'night' and 'moonlight' are mentioned by various characters. Appropriately for the introduction to such a noble place, Puck and the fairy speak in verse. Notice that the fairy's verse has a light and tripping pattern which creates a feeling of movement suited to a fluttering creature. You should look out for this kind of use to which language is put in Shakespeare's plays, for many of his effects were achieved by the use of language alone.

| | | | | |
|---|---|---|---|---|
| 8/25 | Theseus |
| 10/52 | Darkness |
| 17/24 | Moon |

**21  2 1 20  'For Oberon is passing fell . . .'**
Here Puck serves as a kind of chorus by giving the fairy, and therefore the audience, background information about the quarrel between Oberon and Titania. This is an efficient dramatic device for imparting information which the audience will need if they are to make sense of the story without the need for a formal chorus, or storyteller, to stop the action of the play so that they can be brought up to date.

| | |
|---|---|
| 20/23 | Puck |
| 12/22 | Discord |

**22  2 1 28  'And now they never meet . . .'**
Puck tells the fairy about the way in which Oberon and Titania argue about the Indian boy. The argue every time they meet and with such intensity that their elves become frightened and creep away to hide. We see that Oberon and Titania enjoy great power in their world, and we also learn that they have great influence over the world of humans. However, at the end of the play, when the action moves out of the wood and into the world of the humans again, we see that they become transformed into benevolent little spirits.

| | |
|---|---|
| 20/24 | Oberon |
| 19/25 | Titania |
| 21/23 | Discord |
| 19/26 | Nature |

**23  2 1 32  'Either I mistake your shape . . .'**
The fairy begins a catalogue of pranks for which Puck is renowned, which he elaborates with further examples. This serves the function of introducing Puck to us and explaining what sort of character he is, and therefore giving us a good idea of how we might expect him to behave in Shakespeare's play. This is rather clever, because after this we need not trouble ourselves about Puck's motivation for his action, because we already know that he is a 'knavish sprite' and a 'merry wanderer of the night'. Puck's mischief is seen to be unplanned and irrational. He performs his pranks on the spur of the moment and for no other purpose than the amusement he gets from playing practical jokes on humans. Would you say that, in his own way, Puck is mostly a helpful character? Do you think of him as an amiable sort of individual?

| | |
|---|---|
| 21/27 | Puck |
| 22/24 | Discord |

**24  2 1 60  'Ill met by moonlight, proud Titania!'**
Oberon's comment here emphasizes the importance of moonlight as a setting for events in the world of the imagination. His opening line is also a good summary of the situation of the lovers in the play once they enter the wood.

| | |
|---|---|
| 22/25 | Oberon |
| 23/25 | Discord |
| 20/26 | Moon |

**25  2 1 74  'How canst thou thus, . . .'**
Oberon objects to the way Titania is accusing him of secretly harbouring amorous feelings for Hippolyta, especially as she has been romantically involved with Theseus in the past. Not only does this exchange show us that even supernatural and mysterious beings like Oberon and Titania sometimes squabble like jealous lovers, but it strengthens the link between the world of the humans and the world of the fairies – there has clearly been some kind of romantic involvement between Oberon and Hippolyta and between Titania and Theseus.

| | |
|---|---|
| 1/70 | Hippolyta |
| 24/26 | Oberon |
| 20/32 | Theseus |
| 22/26 | Titania |
| 24/27 | Discord |

**26  2 1 81  'These are the forgeries . . .'**
In the second half of this speech of Titania's, we see how the events of the world of the fairies affect the world of humans. Titania lists a catalogue of things which have gone wrong in nature, from rivers which have flooded their banks and rotted the corn in the fields to the weather which has acted out

| | |
|---|---|
| 25/27 | Oberon |
| 25/29 | Titania |
| 10/30 | Imagination |
| 24/32 | Moon |

## Act 2

of season and brought frosts in summer. These unnatural events are caused by the quarrelling between Oberon and Titania. Just as the fairies, for all their power and dignity, are subject to the same emotions as humans, like happiness and jealousy, so events in the fairy world are not remote and separate from the world of humans. This speech therefore reflects an important theme in the play: that the logical, everyday sunlit world is interconnected with the moonlit world of the imagination, where magic and irrationality hold greater sway. Notice also Titania's reference to the way moonlight:

> '. . . washes all the air,
> That rheumatic diseases do abound;'

This is another powerful example of the influence which moonlight has upon the world of man, for the Elizabethans believed that disease was carried upon the air and that it bred in foul vapours. The moonlight, 'Pale in her anger', washes through the air and thereby produces diseases.

*Characters and ideas previous/next comment*

22/27 Nature

---

### 27  2 1 146  'Well, go thy way. . . .'

As Titania leaves with her fairy attendants, Oberon turns to Puck and gives him instructions to find the flower from which he will make the love juice which is to perform such an important part in the play from now on.

It is important to see that this episode gives us a great deal of information about the powers of Oberon and the spirit world in general. This information helps us to understand the kind of spirit which Oberon is. Clearly he is more powerful than Puck, not only because Puck obeys him but because he can see things which Puck cannot, such as the god Cupid flying between heaven and earth. Oberon also has much knowledge of herbs and plants.

Oberon's description of the plant he wants Puck to find is full of references to wonderful and magical things. He remembers the time he heard a mermaid singing and how her song made the rough seas calm and stars shoot across the sky. The mermaid, with the top half of a woman and the tail of a fish, is an interesting image when we think that later on Bottom will be transformed into something which is also half animal and half human, but in his case the other way round, top to tail, or bottom up!

Oberon continues to say how Cupid tried to shoot one of his arrows at a 'fair vestal' enthroned in the west. This was probably a flattering reference by Shakespeare to the 'virgin-queen', Queen Elizabeth I, whose hand in marriage was sought by several suitors without success and who was proud of her virginity. 'Vestal' was the description of the virgin priestesses who tended at the shrine of the Roman deity Vesta, who was the goddess of the home and the hearth.

Oberon explains how Cupid's arrow missed its mark and fell instead upon a small flower, making it change from white to purple, which symbolizes the pain which people in love feel. Because Cupid's arrow did not hit something capable of feeling love its power remained trapped, or 'idle', in the flower, hence the flower's name of 'love-in-idleness'. The flower itself is in fact the common pansy, but Oberon's beautiful description has made the ordinary and commonplace into something wonderful and magical. You should remember that this power which love has was mentioned earlier in the play by Helena, in her speech starting at line 226 in Act One, scene 1, and so we see again how an important theme of the play is reinforced here in this passage spoken by Oberon.

16/41 Bottom
14/30 Helena
26/28 Oberon
23/32 Puck
25/30 Discord
15/56 Mythology
26/28 Nature

---

### 28  2 1 176  'Having once this juice'

Oberon tells Puck how he will put the love juice on Titania's eyes and that when she awakens she will then love the first thing she sees. The animals which Oberon lists – lion, bear, wolf, bull, monkey and ape – were thought of as fierce or fearsome creatures. Contrast these with the creatures which are associated with Titania at the start of Act Three, where an atmosphere is

27/29 Oberon
27/30 Nature

created which is very different to Oberon's vengeful mood here. Whenever the world of nature is mentioned in *A Midsummer Night's Dream* you should look carefully at the kind of images which are used and notice how these are used to reinforce the mood which is being created.

## 29  2 1 176  'Having once this juice'

This speech by Oberon is another example of Shakespeare's use of soliloquy to move the action of the play along by letting us see what a character intends to do next. This also lets the audience know that Oberon's intentions, which could look like cruel revenge, are simply to get the Indian boy back, after which he will release Titania from the spell. We therefore know from the outset that everything will be resolved finally and this dramatic device prevents us from getting too anxious about the fate of Titania and makes sure that the comedy of the situation remains uppermost in our minds.

*Characters and ideas previous/next comment*

28/32  Oberon
26/34  Titania

## 30  2 1 192  'And here am I, and wood . . .'

This comment by Demetrius is a deliberate pun which makes sense when we recall that in Elizabethan times the word 'wood' also meant 'mad'. Demetrius feels that he is being driven mad because he cannot find Hermia and, like Helena at the end of the first scene in Act One, he recognizes that feelings of love make people irrational and unreasonable – 'madly' in love. This explains his unkind behaviour towards Helena here. This is another link between the irrational world of the fairies and the world of humans. The wood, especially at night, is a place where the irrational forces in nature and in humans are brought out. The world of *A Midsummer Night's Dream* is full of the irrational, the magical, the mysterious and the dreamlike. Certainly it seems true that characters who are lost in the fairies' wood are in many ways lost in a world of dreams, where irrational events are commonplace and where what is 'mad' and what is 'normal' become impossibly confused.

12/31  Demetrius
27/31  Helena
27/31  Discord
18/32  Illusion
26/33  Imagination
28/32  Nature

You could be forgiven if you also found the actual story of much of the play confusing but there may be a deliberate reason for the story's apparent confusion. Unlike Shakespeare's other plays, including his other comedies, the figures in *A Midsummer Night's Dream* do not possess great individual subtlety of character. Even the memorable Bottom is something of a caricature rather than a rounded dramatic personality and some of the other characters, especially the lovers, can be confused one with the other, unless their different physical characteristics are emphasized in a performance. This feature of the drama is related to the way Shakespeare makes minimal use of soliloquy, which is common in other plays of his where he wants the audience to 'see into the mind' of a character. This depth of understanding of character is denied to us here and as a result we tend to experience the characters rather more as 'types' and less as individuals. This theme is of course pursued with a vengeance in the episode within the wood, where the lovers themselves seem to become interchangeable. Try to see the characters in *A Midsummer Night's Dream* as labels, or cut-out figures, rather than fully rounded dramatic characters. Notice that this view of the characters makes a difference to the way we would accept them on the stage. For example, consider whether you would be more upset by what happens to each of the lovers if you felt that you had come to 'know' them individually. Shakespeare is in this play dealing very much with 'stock' characters and situations and it seems unlikely that we are expected to respond to them as though they were portraying 'real' people.

Throughout the play we find characters who are defined according to what Shakespeare wishes them to represent – a wise ruler, a passionate lover, a mischievous sprite, and so on. You can gain a good insight into the underlying argument of the play if you think also in this way about the settings used in the play. Why did Shakespeare choose Athens as one setting? What is the point of placing some of the action of the play in a wood (remember the Elizabethan pun on 'wood' – trees, madness and 'wooed').

## Act 2

**31   2 1 243   'I'll follow thee, . . .'**
Helena vows to follow Demetrius, because she loves him so much, even though he has rejected her. This is another one of the many references in the play to love and its power to affect the behaviour of people. It is also another reference to the idea that love is a painful experience, through which various characters in the play proceed towards a harmonious ending, and one which leaves individuals in a state where they are vulnerable to suffering.

| | |
|---|---|
| 30/37 | Demetrius |
| 30/37 | Helena |
| 30/37 | Discord |
| 16/35 | Love |

**32   2 1 245   'Fare thee well, nymph. . . .'**
This whole episode between Helena and Demetrius has been secretly watched by Oberon, who promises that he will turn the tables on them both: Demetrius will chase Helena, who will run away from him. The moonlight wood is just the place for such an unexpected, upside-down situation; it appeals to Oberon and much delights Puck. A few lines further on we see the start of the confusion when Oberon tells Puck to put the love juice into the eyes of the young Athenian; he does not realize that there is another one in the wood and is therefore unprepared for the possibility that Puck might get the two confused. As we know, Puck does make such a mistake. Consider whether other characters such as Lysander, Egeus or Theseus make mistakes and in what ways it could be said that these mistakes occur.

| | |
|---|---|
| 8/55 | Egeus |
| 16/35 | Lysander |
| 29/33 | Oberon |
| 27/35 | Puck |
| 25/42 | Theseus |
| 30/37 | Illusion |
| 26/40 | Moon |
| 30/33 | Nature |

**33   2 1 249   'I know a bank where . . .'**
Oberon's poetic description of Titania's bower is full of beautiful references to the bounty of nature. It brings to mind a sweet and drowsy atmosphere with words like 'luscious' and 'nodding', and reinforces again the magic and beauty of the fairies' world.

| | |
|---|---|
| 32/36 | Oberon |
| 30/40 | Imagination |
| 32/34 | Nature |

It is important to see that this kind of passage is not just decorative material which has been included to make the play more poetic or pretty. The Elizabethan world was still largely a rural one, and images based upon nature would have had an immediate and vivid appeal to the population. Natural imagery would therefore have been a powerful way of making the supernatural world come alive for Shakespeare's audience.

## Scene 2

**34   2 2 1   'Come, now a roundel . . .'**
Songs are an important part of *A Midsummer Night's Dream*. Here, the song 'You spotted snakes with double tongue' is a dramatic device which is used to make Titania fall asleep. The singing, dancing and music all add to the romantic, beautiful, fairy-like quality of the scene. If you were directing this play you would have to make a decision about the kind of music you would think was most appropriate. Often it can be interesting and instructive to look at this aspect of the play in any production which you are able to see. How would you make up your mind about whether a particular piece of music was suitable? You might concentrate on certain aspects of the action to help you decide on this difficult issue, such as the elements of eeriness, magic or comedy. Whether the atmosphere surrounding Bottom's changed appearance should be amusing or fearful would influence many other things and you could usefully decide upon this first.

| | |
|---|---|
| 29/36 | Titania |
| 18/36 | Music |
| 33/36 | Nature |

**35   2 2 51   'O, take the sense, sweet, . . .'**
Lysander explains to Hermia that love has the power to join together two people so that they become almost like one person:

> 'I mean that my heart unto yours is knit,
>   So that but one heart we can make of it.'

This expression of the power of true love summarizes the state to which all the

| | |
|---|---|
| 16/40 | Hermia |
| 32/37 | Lysander |
| 32/36 | Puck |
| 31/37 | Love |

*Characters and ideas previous/next comment*

characters move at the completion of the drama; Lysander's speech also describes another aspect of love, and being in love, which is illustrated in the play.

Lysander is protesting his innocence because Hermia does not want him to sleep too near to her. The word-play, together with Lysander's protestations and Hermia's insistence, makes the situation amusing. Before they sleep they promise to remain loyally in love with each other to the end of their lives, which makes Puck's entry all the more comic, because he promptly mistakes Lysander for Demetrius and puts the love juice on the eyes of the wrong person. We understand immediately that this will make nonsense of the lovers' vows.

### 36  2 2 72  'Through the forest...'

Puck enters to administer the first treatment of the love juice to the humans in the play. Notice the use of rhyming couplets and think about the effect this creates. Say the lines out loud to get a better idea of how the poetry works. As well as reminding you of a kind of song, notice how the verse creates a particular chanting rhythm, like an incantation. If you have read the lines aloud carefully you may also have noticed that there are seven syllables in each line. The Elizabethans regarded seven as a magic number.

Notice also that there are three distinctly different kinds of fairies in this play – Titania's attendants, Puck, and Oberon. Try making a simple list with each of these as a heading, showing how they are similar and different to each other. Useful starting points might be physical attributes such as size, other features such as temperament, attitude towards humans, the extent of their powers, their influence over the elements, where they lived, and where and when they might be found.

| | |
|---|---|
| 33/50 | Oberon |
| 35/48 | Puck |
| 34/47 | Titania |
| 34/47 | Music |
| 34/38 | Nature |

### 37  2 2 90  'Stay though thou kill me,...'

Helena and Demetrius run in, too concerned with their own situation for Demetrius to even notice the woman he is looking for asleep on the stage. He runs on and leaves Helena alone. Helena blames Hermia's beautiful shiny eyes for the fact that Demetrius loves her instead of Helena, and feels that she herself is 'as ugly as a bear'.

The noise that Helena is making presumably wakens Lysander. When he sees Helena he falls instantly in love with her because of the love juice which Puck has just put on his eyes. Notice how his first instinct is irrational – he seeks to kill Demetrius.

| | |
|---|---|
| 31/51 | Demetrius |
| 31/39 | Helena |
| 35/38 | Lysander |
| 31/38 | Discord |
| 32/38 | Illusion |
| 35/47 | Love |

### 38  2 2 117  'Content with Hermia?...'

Lysander declares that he now finds Hermia tedious and loves Helena. The wild speech he uses to say how much he loves Helena is deliberately exaggerated by Shakespeare so that it becomes a parody of a true declaration of love. Notice that he says his love for Helena is based on 'reason'. He repeats this claim several times and this is very ironic, because we know that his love is caused by the love juice, which is something irrational and magical – the very opposite of rationality and reason. We know that Lysander is, in fact, only finding what seem like reasonable excuses for his completely irrational emotions. All four lovers are, in fact, governed by their emotions in this scene, not by any 'reasonable' considerations. This makes Lysander's rejection of Hermia and his vows of love for Helena all the more absurd.

Notice the dramatic use to which language is put here. Compare the way the young men speak to the women when they are in love with them, with the way they speak to them when they think they no longer love them. Notice also the contrast between the language in this scene and that in the scene which follows it – it is the contrast between courtly, artificial speech and more everyday language.

| | |
|---|---|
| 37/39 | Lysander |
| 37/42 | Discord |
| 37/40 | Illusion |
| 36/40 | Nature |

## 34  Act 2

**39  2 2 129  'Wherefore was I to this . . .'**
Helena handles the situation with admirable calmness and rebukes Lysander because she thinks he is mocking her with his vows of love. Again we see a character, here it is Helena, faced with a situation where common sense does not seem to help in understanding the situation which is developing.

| | |
|---|---|
| 37/52 | Helena |
| 38/40 | Lysander |

**40  2 2 151  'Help me, Lysander, . . .'**
Hermia awakes to find Lysander gone. Unbeknown to her, Lysander has woken up with the love juice on his eyes, seen Helena, fallen in love with her and left. When Hermia awakens, therefore, she is alone. We see how Hermia's dream frightened her, for she thought a serpent was eating away her heart whilst Lysander sat by and smiled. We in the audience know that in many ways her dream was true, and this is another example of the power of dreams, or of the imagination, to reveal the truth in a way which reality and reason cannot. We are left at the end of this scene conscious of the feeling that reason is less to be trusted than dreaming. We can also see that the distinction between the reasonable world of daylight and the irrational world of moonlight is becoming more blurred, for Hermia has woken from one nightmare but will soon find that she is in another.

| | |
|---|---|
| 35/49 | Hermia |
| 39/51 | Lysander |
| 38/41 | Illusion |
| 33/41 | Imagination |
| 32/49 | Moon |
| 38/46 | Nature |

*Characters and ideas previous/next comment*

# Act Three

Bottom: *'This is to make an ass of me, to fright me, if they could.'*

## Act 3, scene 1

**41  3 1 1  'Are we all met?'**

Bottom and the other workmen come to rehearse their play and without realizing it pick a spot near to where Titania is still sleeping in her bower. Notice how Quince imagines that certain features of the place, like the grass and some hawthorn, can, with some imagination, be used as though they were a stage in a theatre and a place where the actors would put on costumes. It is another example of how the imagination can easily transform reality and how actors and plays present a different view of 'reality'. This is of course the message which Puck brings to Shakespeare's audience at the end of *A Midsummer Night's Dream*.

The different views of what is 'real' in the play are explored through four different sub-plots which are all intertwined with each other. The story of Theseus's wedding to Hippolyta leads into the second story which is about the young lovers: Lysander, Hermia, Demetrius and Helena. The third sub-plot concerns the quarrel between Oberon and Titania; the fourth is about the workmen's adventures in trying to stage a play. In a sense the fourth story contains within it a fifth story – the plot of the drama *Pyramus and Thisbe*. Each of these stories, in true classical style, has a beginning, a middle and an end. Each story begins at a different point in *A Midsummer Night's Dream* to the others and proceeds at its own pace. The last act of the play brings all the stories together in happy conclusion. Not only does Shakespeare manage to keep all this action running in the play in an interesting and amusing way, but he also makes each story act as a kind of commentary on at least one of the other stories. This complex interweaving and reinterpreting of the themes in the play as a whole is what gives *A Midsummer Night's Dream* such a wonderful dramatic structure. The drama never flags, our interest is continually engaged and when it is performed the play has a strong feeling of 'tightness' and economy – no scene, line, phrase or character ever seems redundant or unnecessary.

*Characters and ideas previous/next comment*

27/42  Bottom
17/44  Quince
16/42  Workmen
40/45  Illusion
40/48  Imagination

---

**42  3 1 75  'Thisbe, the flowers of . . .'**

Bottom is rehearsing his part as Pyramus in the workmen's forthcoming play. He mispronounces 'odours' as 'odorous' and thus completely changes the meaning. This kind of mispronunciation is something which Bottom and Flute often do and it is amusing to search out the examples. These confusions and mispronunciations are appropriate in this scene because all the characters we meet in it are involved in aspects of change. Notice how the workmen's efforts to create a dramatic illusion are confronted with the terrifying reality of Bottom's changed figure later on. The constant mispronunciations are also a skilful device which Shakespeare uses to keep our attention focussed on the kind of language which different characters are speaking – whether poetry or prose – because *A Midsummer Night's Dream* is a play which is as much about ideas as it is about characters. How far would you say the ideas in the play are *more* important than the characters? What evidence could you point to which would support your views?

41/45  Bottom
32/48  Theseus
41/43  Workmen
38/43  Discord

Incidentally, notice how Theseus, who is at the top of the social order, speaks eloquently and with an emphasis on rationality, order and logic, whilst Bottom, who is at the lower end of the social order, speaks in confused, illogical and garbled terms except when describing the world of the imagination; then his words have as much subtlety as those of Theseus.

---

**43  3 1 86  'Most radiant Pyramus, . . .'**

Flute, speaking as Thisbe in the workmen's play, makes an amusing mess of this speech.

42/44  Workmen
42/44  Discord

Notice how the workmen speak in verse when rehearsing their play but prose for the rest of the time. This is another example of the use language serves in Shakespeare's plays to identify the rank of a character or the seriousness of a character's speech. In this example it is particularly interesting to note that although the workmen's play is written in language which conforms to the appearance of poetry, its actual content is of very questionable quality. This clever touch reinforces the suggestion that the honest, uneducated workmen cannot really expect to depict something so sophisticated as a dramatic tragedy without it degenerating into a display of sincere but embarrassing ham acting. Flute, for example, speaks all his part at once, including the cues!

### 44   3 1 91   '"Ninus' tomb", man! . . .'

Quince tries hard to keep his band of amateur actors together but the spectacle of missed cues, wrongly spoken lines, mangled poetry and general uncertainty leads us to smile at the overall mess and the prospect of how this will all appear to the court when performed in front of them. We can see that the workmen's play is unlikely to amount to much in the way of dramatic impact, no matter how long they rehearse!

| | |
|---|---|
| 41/74 | Quince |
| 43/46 | Workmen |
| 43/45 | Discord |

There is an interesting parallel here, in that just as the workmen find the language of drama difficult because it does not suit their normal lives, so the lovers when they emerge from the wood find that their language is unequal to explaining what happened to them.

Shakespeare carefully avoids including this scene we have seen rehearsed in the final version of the workmen's play in Act Five. This is an example of how a careful writer ensures that his theatre audience remains interested at all times and does not come to feel that there are parts of *A Midsummer Night's Dream* that they have seen once already.

### 45   3 1 97   'If I were fair, fair Thisbe, . . .'

Several times in this scene Bottom has already mentioned that actors are often not what they seem to be. With this wonderfully appropriate line, which immediately follows Flute's lines about a horse, Bottom enters wearing the head of an ass. It is even more amusing that Bottom should feel that his friends have run away and left him in the wood as a joke to make him afraid, particularly as it was because of his appearance that they all fled in terror.

| | |
|---|---|
| 42/46 | Bottom |
| 44/47 | Discord |
| 41/46 | Illusion |

### 46   3 1 109   'O Bottom, thou art changed. . . .'

Snout's comment is hilarious. He makes a comment which a person might address to someone who had become different in some subtle, non-obvious way as though the first person were noticing something which others might miss. His comment is also funny because we can imagine the actor delivering it in a dry matter-of-fact manner, and because Bottom has no idea what he is talking about. There is a further amusing reflection here because Bottom, who at the start of the play wanted to act all the parts himself, has now got a part he did not expect!

| | |
|---|---|
| 45/47 | Bottom |
| 44/50 | Workmen |
| 45/48 | Illusion |
| 40/47 | Nature |

### 47   3 1 112   'Bless thee, Bottom! . . .'

Bottom's reply to this comment of Quince's runs along the same lines as the one he made to Snout, and amuses us with its puns on 'ass'. Bottom thinks they are making a fool (or ass) of him when, in fact, he now appears as both a fool and a real ass. The incident also reminds us of the joke on Bottom's name and is doubly amusing because, in order to show his friends that their 'plot' to frighten him has not worked, he begins to sing a song. The sight of Bottom walking up and down singing a song about little birds, oblivious of the fact that he now wears an ass's head, can only seem irrational and ridiculous. Notice how the animals Bottom sings about contrast to others in the play – for example those mentioned by Oberon in Act Two.

| | |
|---|---|
| 46/48 | Bottom |
| 36/48 | Titania |
| 45/48 | Discord |
| 37/54 | Love |
| 36/62 | Music |
| 46/50 | Nature |

Bottom's singing plays an important dramatic part in the action, of course, for it awakens Titania who, because of the love juice on her eyes, immediately falls in love with this creature she sees. The idea that the magical and sensually beautiful Titania can be passionately in love with this strange creature raises the scene's sense of ridiculousness to ludicrous heights. Only

## Act 3

the down-to-earth and perceptive comments of Bottom prevent the scene from becoming a total farce.

Good editions of Shakespeare's works will have notes which explain the meanings of many words which a modern student might find curious or difficult. Sometimes, however, you will find that an apparently 'modern' word had a different meaning in Shakespeare's day, so be prepared to check a troublesome phrase or word even if it seems familiar. Remember, any language changes over a period of time. As a good example, when you come across any of the frequent puns and jokes about Bottom's name, you should remember that in Shakespeare's time the word 'ass' had no contemporary meaning of posterior and the modern (American English) pun on bottom-posterior-backside-ass was therefore impossible.

---

### 48   3 1 135   'Methinks, mistress, you should . . .'

Bottom's observation that Titania has 'little reason' is nearer the mark than either of them suspect and is a good example of Shakespeare's witty humour. Bottom is wonderfully resilient and takes his transformation, and subsequent return to normality, comfortably within his stride! Later on Puck says that he thinks of Bottom as very stupid, but we might think this untrue in the light of Bottom's most perceptive comment here that 'reason and love keep little company together nowadays'. This remark suggests that Bottom has a clearer grasp of reality than any other character in the play and certainly a clearer one than any of the other human characters who stray into the woods. This kind of wisdom is sometimes spoken by the 'fool' characters in Shakespeare's plays, who often speak better sense than some of the characters who are supposed to be wiser than them.

| | |
|---|---|
| 47/59 | Bottom |
| 36/50 | Puck |
| 42/49 | Theseus |
| 47/49 | Titania |
| 47/51 | Discord |
| 46/52 | Illusion |
| 41/53 | Imagination |

This puzzling contrast between Bottom's apparent stupidity and his evident folk wisdom is only one of many such puzzles in the play; the fairies can be good or evil; everyday reality can be misleading whilst illusions can expose truth; Theseus seems powerful but his authority has strict limits; and what seems irrational can make greater sense than logic can explain. Contrasts are also drawn between disorder and harmony, love and hate, town and country, dream and reality. *A Midsummer Night's Dream* makes it clear, especially at the end, that any attempts by us to fully unravel these puzzling contrasts will make us as much an ass as Bottom. The play is supposed to leave the audience uncertain. This is the point of Shakespeare's plot. The play encourages the audience to recognize the value of their imagination, of the irrational and emotional part of their nature, and not to seek forever to understand everything through reason alone.

---

### 49   3 1 192   'Come, wait upon him. . . .'

In Titania's short speech in which she asks her fairies to accompany Bottom to her bower we find another interesting reference to the moon. Several times in the play we find the moon associated with sadness or anger; and the moon is often seen as changeable, unpredictable and swiftly flying. Here the sad moon has a 'watery eye' as though 'Lamenting some enforcèd chastity'. The idea that 'enforcèd chastity' is sad was first introduced by Theseus at the start of the play when he was talking to Hermia and these kinds of echoes help to bind the play together as one dramatic whole.

| | |
|---|---|
| 40/52 | Hermia |
| 48/55 | Theseus |
| 48/59 | Titania |
| 40/63 | Moon |

*Characters and ideas previous/next comment*

# Scene 2

**50  3 2 6  'My mistress with a monster . . .'**
Puck, acting again as a kind of chorus, brings Oberon up to date with events in the play. The speech contains some fine images, such as the one around line 20 where Puck compares the workmen who are rushing about in a confused and bewildered state with startled jackdaws and geese which 'Sever themselves and madly sweep the sky' at the sound of a hunter's gunfire.

There is a great deal of animal imagery in the play not least, of course, to do with Bottom's transformation. There is an interesting echo here with the Athenian background to this play. Many of the main characters names are Greek, as is the setting, and the wood itself has strong overtones of Greek mythology. In Shakespeare's play the wood is placed just outside Athens but in its character it shares many features with the famous labyrinth of Crete. Young men and young virgins visited both places to undergo frightening ordeals and both places contained a monster which was half man, half beast. The magic and mystery of Greek mythology runs strongly through the magic of Oberon and the spirit world, with its constant changing of one thing into another and its constantly confusing mixture of the real and the imagined. If we remember that Bottom's name is connected with the spool which a weaver used to wind thread around, we may be reminded of the way in which, in the legend of the Minotaur, Theseus used such a device to find his way out of the labyrinth.

Another echo of the same group of legends occurs at the end of Shakespeare's play, when we are told that the first entertainment being offered at Theseus's wedding feast is *The Battle with the Centaurs*. It is interesting to note that in the topsy-turvy world of the wood, Bottom's transformation gives him the appearance of a kind of upside-down Centaur, which in Greek mythology was a creature with the top half of a man and the bottom half of a horse.

*Characters and ideas previous/next comment*

| | |
|---|---|
| 36/51 | Oberon |
| 48/51 | Puck |
| 46/53 | Workmen |
| 47/53 | Nature |
| 6/59 | Order |

**51  3 2 136  'Demetrius loves her, . . .'**
Lysander's comment to Helena is immediately followed by a declaration of profoundest love from Demetrius, phrased in the most exaggerated and ridiculous terms! This moment, like much of the rest of the scene, emphasizes the confused and upside-down nature of the world within the wood. We also see that the contradictions and the anger of the four lovers become more pronounced as the scene continues. The fact that much of this confusion comes about because of comic mistakes only serves to make it more amusing for Puck and for the audience. Unlike the lovers, we know, like Puck, that Oberon is going to resolve everything eventually and so we tend to ignore the potentially tragic outcomes which are so upsetting for the lovers.

| | |
|---|---|
| 37/53 | Demetrius |
| 40/53 | Lysander |
| 50/55 | Oberon |
| 50/55 | Puck |
| 48/52 | Discord |

**52  3 2 177  'Dark night that from . . .'**
The entry of Hermia signals the climax of this, the longest scene in the play. She is happy that at last she has found Lysander although this quickly turns to bewilderment at the reaction of the other three lovers. She rounds angrily on Helena about a hundred lines further on when she suspects that Helena has stolen Lysander away from her. Helena's reaction is that the other three are conspiring to make a fool of her. Lysander hates Hermia and loves Helena; Demetrius, woken from sleep and influenced by the love juice, now loves Helena; all of which Helena sees as a cruel joke.

| | |
|---|---|
| 39/54 | Helena |
| 49/54 | Hermia |
| 20/56 | Darkness |
| 51/53 | Discord |
| 48/53 | Illusion |

**53  3 2 260  'Hang off, thou cat, . . .'**
Both Lysander and Demetrius are, of course, equally convinced that they are the better person and are more in love than the other. They hurl abuse both at each other and also at the women whom they so recently thought of as goddesses and it appears as though there may soon be an actual fight between them. Whilst we in the audience can find the antics of the two men amusing, we should also notice how powerful a hold their illusions have on them and how it is these illusions, not the people themselves, which are producing this painful but funny situation.

| | |
|---|---|
| 51/57 | Demetrius |
| 51/55 | Lysander |
| 50/69 | Workmen |
| 52/54 | Discord |
| 52/57 | Illusion |
| 48/65 | Imagination |
| 50/55 | Nature |

## Act 3

The problem for the characters in *A Midsummer Night's Dream* is, of course, that they cannot tell when things are real and when things are illusory; everything seems equally real to them. This is an interesting puzzle for us in the audience, for we think that *we* know the difference between illusion and reality, which is why we can laugh at the characters in the play, but in fact this feeling is being produced in us only because we have 'gone along with' the illusion of the play and accepted the actions of the actors on the stage as those of believable characters. The humour in this scene is therefore quite subtle. Shakespeare's plays often contain an examination of the relationship between reality and imagination and these are frequently treated in a humorous way. Another good example in this play is, of course, the considerable confusion and amusement which surrounds the workmen's rehearsal and performance of *Pyramus and Thisbe*.

---

### 54  3 2 306  'Good Hermia, do not be . . .'

Just as we have seen the irrational change in the feelings of Demetrius, who now claims to love Helena, so we see a breakup of a lifelong friendship between Hermia and Helena. Hermia is upset because she suspects her friend of mocking her because she is not as tall as Helena; she retorts by calling Helena a 'painted maypole'. We can see that this spiteful and petty quarrel is completely irrational, which is in keeping with the way of things within the wood.

| | |
|---|---|
| 52/55 | Helena |
| 52/67 | Hermia |
| 53/55 | Discord |
| 47/55 | Love |

It is interesting to note that, with the exception of Titania, who is a character from the spirit world, it is only the male lovers whose judgement is impaired by exposure to the love juice. The actions of the women here are therefore a result of the behaviour of the men and are not caused by the women's own illogical attitudes. This is a neat inversion of the traditional stereotype, in which it is the women who are depicted as emotional and irrational and the men who are characterized as cool and logical.

---

### 55  3 2 354  'Thou seest these lovers . . .'

Oberon is concerned that Lysander and Demetrius may actually become involved in a fight with each other. It is part of Oberon's responsibility to be kind and helpful to humans, after his fashion, and so he regards the prospect of a fight with great seriousness. He orders Puck to go and make sure that both the young lovers get lost and do not meet up with each other, and that they eventually become exhausted and fall asleep. Puck is then to put the antidote to the love juice on Lysander's eyes so that he is no longer blinded by illusions. Notice how Oberon behaves here rather like Theseus does with regard to acting with responsibility. Do you think Oberon or Theseus is the more important character in the play? Try to decide how you reached your conclusion.

| | |
|---|---|
| 32/65 | Egeus |
| 54/67 | Helena |
| 53/57 | Lysander |
| 51/59 | Oberon |
| 51/56 | Puck |
| 49/63 | Theseus |
| 54/57 | Discord |
| 54/59 | Love |
| 53/56 | Nature |

If you read this part of the play carefully you will notice that Oberon does not tell Puck to put any of the antidote on the eyes of Demetrius. Can you think why he has not told Puck to administer the antidote to him? You should be able to come to a conclusion about this if you think back to what Oberon said in Act Two, scene one, when he had overheard the conversation between Demetrius and Helena. Reading this again should enable you to understand Oberon's way of helping humans – it means that he thinks of *how* events should come out if they are to be what in his judgement is fair. This is the identical situation which Theseus faced at the start of the play in deciding how best to help Egeus with his problem. In the particular case here in Act Three, Oberon's actions mean that Demetrius will therefore continue to love Helena.

---

### 56  3 2 378  'My fairy lord, this must . . .'

Puck reminds Oberon that dawn, 'Aurora's harbinger', is approaching quickly as the 'swift dragons' of night speed on their way. He also mentions the traditional Elizabethan superstition that 'damned spirits' must return to their burial places under water and at crossroads. The notion that unhappy or

| | |
|---|---|
| 55/57 | Puck |
| 52/77 | Darkness |
| 27/57 | Mythology |
| 55/59 | Nature |

troubled spirits were buried at crossroads is interesting, for in many ways the four lovers have now to return to the parting of the ways at the edge of the wood, having been sorely troubled by their visit to the spirit world of the imagination. Notice, though, that Oberon is quick to point out that he and his fairies in the wood are not 'damned' but are 'spirits of another sort', which reassures us that the ordeals of the lovers have not been prompted by evil spirits.

**57   3 2 440   'Cupid is a knavish lad'**
The amusement of this part of the play comes as much from the bewildered and exhausted state of the women as from the behaviour of the men. Lysander and Demetrius see themselves as acting in ways which are noble, rational, determined and honourable. In fact they are being led a merry dance by the mischievous Puck and we see them as ridiculous figures of fun. The women, driven frantic by the bizarre behaviour of the men, weary of the chase through the wood, are tattered and soaked with dew. There are therefore several kinds of 'madness' illustrated for us at the end of this scene. Puck himself delights in his own wild and irrational behaviour. How far are you able to like Puck as a character? Think carefully about the things which influence you in deciding upon your answer.

| | |
|---|---|
| 53/65 | Demetrius |
| 55/67 | Lysander |
| 56/58 | Puck |
| 55/58 | Discord |
| 53/59 | Illusion |
| 56/70 | Mythology |

**58   3 2 448   'On the ground'**
During this scene we have seen the action move through complicated confusions, bitterness and argument, shouting, running and near violence. This final speech by Puck, with its references to traditional country folklore, closes the action on a note of tranquillity as Lysander, Demetrius, Helena and Hermia all fall asleep. Notice how this atmosphere prepares the audience for the dramatic contrast of a change of pace with which the next scene starts when the comedy begins afresh with the reappearance of the still ass-headed Bottom.

| | |
|---|---|
| 57/59 | Puck |
| 57/59 | Discord |

# Act Four

Puck: 'Now when thou wakest with thine own fool's eyes peep.'

# Act 4, scene 1

**59  4 1 1  'Come, sit thee down . . .'**

This scene begins with Titania and Bottom falling asleep just like the characters at the end of the last scene. Titania is still at this stage deeply in love with Bottom. She strokes his cheeks, puts roses on his brow and kisses his ears. This absurdly comic but beautiful scene is touching because the characters are sincere and innocent. Bottom's polite requests for food and entertainment from the fairies are amusing because of the innocent way he asks for things which would be completely appropriate only if he really were an ass. This point is made more funny when Bottom, suggesting that he has a 'good ear' (which is another lovely joke) for beautiful, sweet music, asks for a tune on 'the tongs and the bones', which seem to have been crude rustic percussion instruments!

The atmosphere at the start of this scene continues that at the end of the last scene, with the action of the play turning away from the chaos of illusion towards the harmony of the final act. The play is now moving towards a restoration of order and harmony. The first stage in this process is that all the major characters involved must submit to sleep (as some already have at the end of the last scene) whilst Puck and Oberon begin to exercise their magical influence in the world of nature. About sixty lines into this scene, we find Oberon explaining this process to Puck:

> 'And now I have the boy I will undo
> This hateful imperfection of her eyes.'

Bottom, like Titania, is to be released from enchantment so that, along with the other Athenians, he will remember the events in the wood as only 'the fierce vexation of a dream'. This dream world represents in many ways the illusions created by love and it can, like love itself, be a painful as well as an enjoyable experience.

Bottom is a central character in much of the dreaming and illusion which goes on in the play, being the victim of the most powerful and beautiful dream and the moving force behind wanting to create the most obvious illusion – the play within the play. Also, the main theme of *Pyramus and Thisbe* is concerned with the foolishness and freedom of love, a theme which is also central to *A Midsummer Night's Dream*.

*Characters and ideas previous/next comment*

| | |
|---|---|
| 48/62 | Bottom |
| 55/61 | Oberon |
| 58/61 | Puck |
| 49/60 | Titania |
| 58/63 | Discord |
| 57/63 | Illusion |
| 55/60 | Love |
| 56/60 | Nature |
| 50/60 | Order |

---

**60  4 1 39  'Sleep thou, and I will wind . . .'**

The imagery of nature and natural things is used to beautiful effect here, where Titania likens her embrace of the sleeping Bottom to the way plants wind around each other:

> 'So doth the woodbine the sweet honeysuckle
> Gently entwist; the female ivy so
> Enrings the barky fingers of the elm.'

These powerful images of harmony and support accurately sum up a great deal about the Elizabethan's view of the relationship between the mysterious world of nature and the everyday world of mankind.

| | |
|---|---|
| 59/63 | Titania |
| 59/65 | Love |
| 59/61 | Nature |
| 59/61 | Order |

---

**61  4 1 45  'Welcome, good Robin. . . .'**

Oberon welcomes Puck, the mischievous sprite, with the name of Robin. In country lore Robin Goodfellow was the same as Puck, and we should not miss this gentle hint at the change in the behaviour of Oberon and how he uses Puck, for their power and magic will now be turned towards restoring harmony. Puck has consistently been the cause of confusion and mischief. From now on he will, as Oberon promises, be a spirit 'of another sort', a Robin Goodfellow.

| | |
|---|---|
| 59/63 | Oberon |
| 59/84 | Puck |
| 60/66 | Nature |
| 60/62 | Order |

## Act 4

| | Characters and ideas previous/next comment |
|---|---|

**62  4 1 82  'Music, ho! Music such as . . .'**

Throughout the play music, because of its use of harmony, is often referred to when other forms of harmony are being suggested – harmony between two lovers or within the state. Here, the use of music in the scene symbolizes the way the action of the play is returning from discord to harmony. The pun on the word 'charmeth' suggests that the music will be so beautiful that it will act like a charm, like magic; also it will charm away the confusions in the mind of Bottom and act as an antidote to Puck's magic. References to music and harmony occur in the words spoken by several different speakers throughout the rest of this scene. Notice how the dance of Oberon and Titania also has magic power; dancing is used several times in *A Midsummer Night's Dream* in this way.

| | |
|---|---|
| 59/68 | Bottom |
| 47/63 | Music |
| 61/63 | Order |

**63  4 1 102  'Go, one of you; . . .'**

The atmosphere created by the tender music and dancing of the reunited Oberon and Titania is rudely shattered by the clamorous entry of Theseus to the sound of horns and the baying of hunting dogs. Dreaming and illusion belong to the night and with the arrival of day they have been scattered. The lovers will now untangle their relationships in the starker illumination of daylight. This moment returns the action of the play from the mischief and magic of the fairy world to the world of humans.

| | |
|---|---|
| 61/67 | Oberon |
| 55/64 | Theseus |
| 60/84 | Titania |
| 59/70 | Discord |
| 59/66 | Illusion |
| 49/70 | Moon |
| 62/64 | Music |
| 62/64 | Order |

**64  4 1 118  'My hounds are bred . . .'**

Although Theseus uses his hounds for hunting he says that they are not very good at chasing things and that he mainly likes them for the way their cries produce a kind of harmony. Theseus may be a very practical and down-to-earth ruler but he prefers less effective hunting hounds which are 'matched' to ones which are not in accord, or harmony, with each other. Harmony is more important to Theseus than outstanding qualities of other kinds.

| | |
|---|---|
| 63/65 | Theseus |
| 63/81 | Music |
| 63/65 | Order |

**65  4 1 153  'Enough, enough – my lord, . . .'**

Egeus, speaking for the last time in the play, asks Theseus for the judgement of the law upon the head of Lysander. Although Egeus consistently has right on his side, by now we recognize that his behaviour is not very reasonable. Notice this contrast between the 'reason' of Egeus and Theseus's 'unreasonable' but compassionate judgement that Hermia shall marry Lysander. This marks the establishment of a new and better kind of order in the world within Shakespeare's play. The play now moves into a realm where the factual reality of everyday experience is tempered by an awareness of the mysteries of the world of the imagination, where people better understand that the frontier between reality and illusion is not clear cut.

Notice that Demetrius's reply to Egeus marks a complete change in the tone of the speech used by the lovers. Whilst they were in the wood the speech of the lovers, especially Demetrius and Lysander, was affected by great hyperbole (or exaggeration). We in the audience understood this as reflecting a lack of sincerity, which we nevertheless understood because we knew that the effect was being produced by love juice and we were not therefore hearing the 'real' characters speak. The language of hyperbole is now replaced by speech devoid of ornament, which suggests the complete sincerity of the speaker. Significantly, we hear no more hyperbole from any of the lovers who have spent time within the madness of the wood. It is as though they have been purged of false sentiment by their experiences. This is an important idea, because it is exactly what Elizabethans expected drama to do for the audience – purge them of their passions by exposing them to plays which depicted characters suffering great passions.

| | |
|---|---|
| 57/66 | Demetrius |
| 55/0 | Egeus |
| 64/70 | Theseus |
| 53/68 | Imagination |
| 60/66 | Love |
| 64/69 | Order |

## Act 4

**66  4 1 186  'These things seem small . . .'**
Demetrius explains how the experiences through which he has just come seem to him 'Like far-off mountains turnèd into clouds'. This powerful image is wonderfully appropriate, for at a distance far-off mountains often do look like clouds and it is sometimes difficult to tell apart distant clouds and mountain ranges. Also the image evokes the idea that mountains, things which seem powerfully solid, can appear as insubstantial and indistinct. Hermia says that she feels as though she has been seeing double. These ideas suggest that love, dreams and irrationality are the other half of, or another appearance of, the real, logical and common sense world.

| | |
|---|---|
| 65/67 | Demetrius |
| 63/67 | Illusion |
| 65/67 | Love |
| 61/67 | Nature |

---

**67  4 1 190  'And I have found Demetrius, . . .'**
This comment by Helena is important, all the more so for being easily overlooked. She says that Demetrius is now 'Mine own and not mine own'. Demetrius goes on to say that he is not sure whether he is awake or not and that he is unsure as to whether he is still in a dream or not. Hermia comments that she now seems to see things with '. . . parted eye, When everything seems double'.

| | |
|---|---|
| 66/79 | Demetrius |
| 55/0 | Helena |
| 54/0 | Hermia |
| 57/79 | Lysander |
| 63/84 | Oberon |
| 66/68 | Illusion |
| 66/69 | Love |
| 66/70 | Nature |

These important remarks should remind us that Demetrius is still acting under the influence of the love juice which, having once been applied, is in his case never removed. Helena now has her lover back again but only because of Oberon's magic. The other two lovers – Lysander and Hermia – are free of Oberon's magic and therefore truly in a love entirely of their own making. Helena's observation contains more truth than she realizes. This is another example of one of the play's many ironies.

Tracing out the several sub-plots of the play can be interesting, as the whole play is made up of these. Here, for example, one of the plots reaches what amounts to its end, for the lovers' relationships are now resolved. Notice how this does not affect the momentum of the drama as a whole, because of the careful way Shakespeare has woven the different plots together. This 'cutting' from one story to another might strike you as a rather modern cinematic technique, but it has, in fact, a long pedigree. Shakespeare retains the audience's interest and involvement by interweaving the plots together so that they 'comment' on each other at many points, or contain echoes of each other. This is reminiscent of the way Titania described the intertwining of plants at the beginning of scene four and is an example of how skilfully Shakespeare has woven the story, characters, language, settings and imagery into one dramatic whole.

---

**68  4 1 209  '. . . The eye of man hath not heard, . . .'**
Most critics agree that this speech of Bottom's, which he makes upon waking from his dream, is a parody of a section in St Paul:

| | |
|---|---|
| 62/76 | Bottom |
| 67/70 | Illusion |
| 65/76 | Imagination |

> 'But as it is written, eye hath not seen, nor ear heard,
> neither have entered into the heart of man, the things
> which God hath prepared for them that love him.'
> (I Corinthians ii 9)

Bottom attempts to convey the wonder of his dream in a garbled form of this:

> 'The eye of man hath not heard, the ear of man hath not seen,
> man's hand is not able to taste, his tongue to conceive, nor
> his heart to report, what my dream was!'

Elizabethans were much more familiar with the Bible than most people are today and it seems very likely that Shakespeare's audience would have recognized so close a parallel between the two pieces, and would probably also have found it amusing that such a coarse and rustic figure as Bottom could only manage to speak words from such a holy book by turning them upside down. Bottom's back to front rendering of the Bible is, of course, typical of the glorious muddle he usually ends up in and the way he often mixes up his words.

Notice that Bottom believes that his wonderful dream should be written down as a ballad by Peter Quince. Bottom is suggesting to us that the most effective way to capture and understand the confusing world of the irrational, the world of magic and of dreams, is through poetry, song or, as in *A Midsummer Night's Dream* itself, through a theatrical drama. Importantly, Bottom suggests that his ballad shall be called 'Bottom's Dream', because it has 'no bottom'. Dreams are based upon insubstantial 'nothings' and therefore have 'no bottom' – no solid foundation in reality – and this is exactly true of Shakespeare's play itself. This idea of the insubstantial nature of drama is discussed again in comments 70 and 86. Just like Bottom's dream, the play is powerfully true in a way which escapes attempts to fully understand it and, in this sense, it is as unfathomable as Bottom's dream in its depth of meaning.

## Scene 2

**69  4 2 1  'Have you sent to Bottom's house? . . .'**
This brief scene acts as a dramatic boundary between the complex action of the last scene, where the lovers awake from their sleep, and the next and final scene in the play, where the action of the play is brought to a harmonious close.

The scene contains the usual mix-ups which we have come to associate with the workmen. Quince causes amusement by confusing 'paragon' and 'paramour' and Starveling says that Bottom has been 'transported'. Starveling means that Bottom has gone somewhere else and is therefore not to be found, but his remark is an ironic and unintentionally witty comment. Lovers were supposed to be 'transported' by love – that is, to have their feelings moved to another, higher, realm. Because we know what has been happening to Bottom in the wood, we understand how this is true in a way which Starveling does not mean.

When Bottom appears, to the delight of the others, it is to announce that their play has been put on the short list for the entertainments, and rehearsal begins in earnest. Bottom appears to be about to tell his friends about his wonderful adventures but, with a delightful swerve of direction, he instead fires off instructions for the preparations which need to be made.

*Characters and ideas previous/next comment*

53/74  Workmen
67/70  Love
65/70  Order

# Act Five

Quince: 'Gentles, perchance you wonder at this show . . .'

## Act 5, scene 1

**70  5 1 2  'More strange than true. . . .'**

As we join this scene, Theseus and Hippolyta are discussing the stories which the young lovers have told them. Theseus feels that the lovers have been suffering from overheated imaginations, no doubt caused by the intensity of their passions. He likens them to poets whose visions exist on the very edge of sanity:

> 'The lunatic, the lover, and the poet
> Are of imagination all compact.'

Like much of the rest of *A Midsummer Night's Dream* this speech by Theseus contains some subtle observations by Shakespeare about the nature of artistic reality and how it fits against the everyday world of human experience. Notice the interesting, ambiguous mention of 'lunatic', a word which stems from *luna*, the moon. We in the audience know that any play depends on the creation of a special kind of illusion where the audience 'pretend', along with the actors, that something 'real' is going on. The other important point being made is that a person should strive for balance in his or her outlook, because to be driven entirely by imagination or entirely by what is rational can lead to a distorted view of the world – a kind of blindness.

A few lines further on we find Theseus describing how the lover can imagine beauty where none is present. He talks about the face of a gipsy – 'a brow of Egypt' – as an example. We must remember that a dark complexion, especially a Moorish or African one, was not considered beautiful by the Elizabethans, who intensely distrusted such people because of their different religious beliefs, which they considered 'heathen'. Thus the passion of the lover, says Theseus, can bring into existence beauty where none is really present. This is a characteristic the lover shares with the imagination of the poet, who:

> 'Doth glance from heaven to earth, from earth to heaven.
> And as imagination bodies forth
> The forms of things unknown, the poet's pen
> Turns them to shapes, and gives to airy nothing
> A local habitation and a name.'

As well as being a concise and rational explanation of how the imagination of the lovers could have conjured up their fantastic experiences in the wood, this is a wonderful description of Shakespeare's own art in *A Midsummer Night's Dream*. If we were to accept literally what Theseus is saying in this speech, then all of the cast of the play would presumably disappear into 'airy nothing'! Until the play is performed, or until we read it, this is of course quite true – Theseus, Oberon, Bottom and the rest do not 'exist' except as imaginary, dramatic characters.

There is a further neat irony in Theseus's dismissal of the lovers' stories as 'antique fables', for as one of the play's mythological characters, what else is he but just such a thing himself?

*Characters and ideas previous/next comment*

| | |
|---|---|
| 25/71 | Hippolyta |
| 65/73 | Theseus |
| 63/72 | Discord |
| 68/71 | Illusion |
| 69/71 | Love |
| 63/85 | Moon |
| 57/75 | Mythology |
| 67/84 | Nature |
| 69/73 | Order |

---

**71  5 1 23  'But all the story . . .'**

Hippolyta is not as convinced as Theseus that the experiences of the lovers can be explained by some kind of derangement brought about by their intense passion. Although she cannot explain herself how this might be so, Hippolyta seems to sense that the lovers have experienced something genuinely strange and bizarre.

| | |
|---|---|
| 70/77 | Hippolyta |
| 70/73 | Illusion |
| 70/78 | Love |

---

**72  5 1 44  'The Battle with the Centaurs, . . .'**

As Theseus reads through the list of entertainments on offer for the evening, he eventually reaches the workmen's own description of their play. Again we see how the confusion of opposites causes amusement as we in the audience struggle, with the courtiers, to make sense of how something can be 'tedious' whilst also being 'brief' and 'tragical' whilst causing 'mirth'. But because we know more than the characters in the play, we can understand how it is

| | |
|---|---|
| 70/74 | Discord |

possible to reconcile these seemingly contradictory things and we can do so whilst at the same time sharing the laughter of the courtiers.

---

### 73   5 1 61   'A play there is, my lord, . . .'
Philostrate adds to the amusement of this scene by observing that the workmen's play is indeed 'brief', being only some ten words long, but is so bad that in his opinion it is ten words *too* long, and is therefore extremely 'tedious'! The educated and sophisticated Philostrate is unable to appreciate ham acting and tells of how he cried with laughter at the poorness of the play when he saw it in rehearsal.

We are able to see that this is not true for Theseus who, as a humane and perceptive ruler, is able to accept the clumsy but sincere drama in the spirit in which it is presented. Theseus knows that the workmen are not as well fitted for their task as other more professional and polished performers may be, but he prizes their other qualities more highly. We have seen this characteristic in Theseus before, when he spoke about his hunting hounds. Like the audience as it has watched *A Midsummer Night's Dream*, Theseus has come to know that the most valuable aspects of things may not be the ones which immediately meet the eye.

When Queen Elizabeth I journeyed around England she was often presented with entertainments by her subjects and it is said that she always accepted them very graciously, no matter how amateurish or clumsy. It is often suggested that the attitude of Theseus to the workmen's play was therefore intended as another compliment by Shakespeare to his monarch.

|       |          |
|-------|----------|
| 70/77 | Theseus  |
| 71/76 | Illusion |
| 70/81 | Order    |

---

### 74   5 1 108   'If we offend it is . . .'
Quince begins the workmen's play with a hopelessly mangled speech in which he gets all the punctuation – 'points' – wrong and makes it mean the opposite of what it is suppposed to. The courtiers find this hilarious and throughout the whole performance they repeatedly make unkind comments about the workmen's acting.

You should be sensitive to what is going on in this part of the scene. The courtiers laugh at the workmen's attempts to produce a noble and tragic play, which should be very grand and majestic, because their attempt is ham fisted and unskilled. The laughter of the courtiers is not meant kindly, particularly that of the young lovers. Their laughter stems from ridicule and is therefore based on a condescending and callous judgement of what they see.

We in the audience also laugh at the performance of *Pyramus and Thisbe*, but for somewhat different reasons. Firstly, we do not see an anonymous collection of poorly educated 'hard-handed men', as Philostrate has called them. We see Bottom, Quince, Snout, Flute and Snug. We have come to feel rather fond of these bumbling but kind-hearted and sincere characters. Whilst we can laugh at the amateurish performance, our amusement is warm, not barbed. The performance that we in the audience see has something rather touching about its sincerity.

|       |          |
|-------|----------|
| 44/75 | Quince   |
| 69/75 | Workmen  |
| 72/75 | Discord  |

---

### 75   5 1 143   'Anon comes Pyramus . . .'
Instead of impressing the audience with what is clearly intended to be powerful and beautiful poetry, this speech by Quince is delivered in such inappropriate language that instead it reduces them to laughter because it sounds so absurd. The technical term for this is bathos, a term used to describe what happens when there is a sudden descent from the exalted or wonderful to the ordinary or trite. A particularly good example of the inappropriate use of language in this speech comes when Quince tries to use alliteration to describe Pyramus's death '– with bloody, blameful blade –/He bravely broached his boiling bloody breast', and again at the death of Thisbe, who 'His dagger drew, and died'.

|       |           |
|-------|-----------|
| 74/0  | Quince    |
| 74/80 | Workmen   |
| 74/76 | Discord   |
| 70/84 | Mythology |

## Act 5

As the workmen's play continues there are many more examples of the inappropriate uses of language and we see the characters continually stepping outside their part to explain what is happening to the audience.

### 76  5 1 181  'No, in truth sir, he should not. . . .'

This wonderful moment is a good example of one of the things which make the performance of *Pyramus and Thisbe* so funny. Bottom, overhearing Theseus's comment, steps out of character to address the audience directly and explain something. The humour comes from the fact that this reveals that Bottom has little idea of how important it is in a drama to maintain the sense of reality which the actors create. Also Bottom has in fact misunderstood Theseus's witticism and has taken his remark wrongly. Much of the humour of the workmen's play comes from the way they perform it in the most deadly seriousness – none more so than Bottom – and yet both we and the court find it impossible to take such an amateurishly performed and awfully written drama seriously at all. *Pyramus and Thisbe*, as performed for us here, is in fact an excellent example of how a play can be *so* dreadfully bad that it becomes brilliantly funny.

| 68/78 | Bottom |
| 75/77 | Discord |
| 73/77 | Illusion |
| 68/77 | Imagination |

### 77  5 1 207  'This is the silliest stuff . . .'

Hippolyta finds the workmen's play to be so poorly performed that she cannot accept the characters as believable. What precisely does she find objectionable about the play do you think? Is it perhaps the story, or the characters, or the language or the unskilled acting? When you have decided on your answer to this, stop for a moment to consider what it is about the workmen's play which we in the audience therefore find amusing.

| 71/0  | Hippolyta |
| 73/81 | Theseus |
| 56/85 | Darkness |
| 76/78 | Discord |
| 76/78 | Illusion |
| 76/85 | Imagination |

Theseus points out to Hippolyta that the audience must exercise its imagination to compensate for any lack of polish on the part of the actors – even the best actors, he says, are 'but shadows', which rely on the willing participation of the audience to lend them dramatic substance. This is the point which the workmen have missed in their continual interruption of their play to explain things to the audience. By stepping outside their characters the workmen are actually destroying the illusion which they are so keen to create.

Again, we see how *A Midsummer Night's Dream* stresses the important role which the imagination plays in the way people understand their world and how they use their imagination to define what is 'real' in the emotional sense of what is most 'meaningful' to them. All emotions, like love and hatred, are 'real' for the people experiencing them, but cannot be seen, touched or tasted. *A Midsummer Night's Dream* therefore seems to be suggesting that to rely therefore on only those tangible things which can be explained by the use of logic and reason may lead us to be blind to an important part of being human. How, and how far, has Shakespeare managed to convince you of this argument?

### 78  5 1 283  'O wherefore, nature, . . .'

This completely overacted death speech by Bottom is one of the most ludicrous episodes in the workmen's play. Bottom tangles up the ending and thereby wrecks his already bad verse, but takes himself so seriously that the audience is frequently reduced to laughter at this point. It is important to see, however, that there is something more subtle happening beneath the surface humour. The drama of *Pyramus and Thisbe* actually depicts a situation in which the lovers could have found themselves, were it not for the intervention of Oberon, when it looked as though Lysander and Demetrius might fight.

| 76/0  | Bottom |
| 77/80 | Discord |
| 77/83 | Illusion |
| 71/80 | Love |

Just as Bottom's speech is a parody of good drama, so we can perhaps think of more modern examples which produce the same effect. Can you think of other kinds of drama which, because of their stilted style or amateurish and unconvincing settings and acting, unintentionally become funny or embarrassing? To begin with, think of some television series or soap operas.

In this speech Bottom displays his inability to understand the way drama works. He gets mixed up between the illusory world which he and his fellow workmen are trying to create and the real world outside their play. The confusions which result from the workmen periodically stepping outside their play to explain things to their audience are, however, no more ridiculous than the confusion which the lovers became entangled in within the wood. It is ironic therefore that the lovers are rather sneering at times whilst watching the workmen's play. Just as Bottom cannot see that reality has no place within the performance of *Pyramus and Thisbe*, so the lovers have been unable to understand that reality has a questionable part to play in the way people fall in love with each other.

---

**79  5 1 299  'No die, but an ace for him; . . .'**
Demetrius and Lysander exchange jokes about the awfulness of the play. A 'die' is one of a pair of dice and the lowest score possible on a die is a 'one', which was known as an 'ace'. Their puns and sarcasm are at the expense of Bottom's final line. We, who remember how these two courtiers behaved in the wood, can see the irony in what they suppose to be their wit and sophistication.

| | |
|---|---|
| 67/0 | Demetrius |
| 67/0 | Lysander |

---

**80  5 1 316  'Asleep, my love?'**
Flute, as Thisbe, begins a speech upon finding Pyramus's dead body. The humour comes from the language, which is hilarious because of its clumsiness. The intention is clearly to impress us with delicate and moving love poetry, but this is instantly made impossible by the words used to describe Pyramus:

> 'These lily lips,
> This cherry nose,
> These yellow cowslip cheeks'

The bad poetry of the workmen's play reaches its most ridiculous and comical extent when Thisbe turns her attention to describing the eyes of her love Pyramus:

> 'His eyes were green as leeks.'

We can imagine that Flute, as an amateurish actor, probably delivers these lines in an unskilled way. The overall effect would be completely unconvincing, shattering any dramatic illusion that such doggerel might conceivably have created. A few lines later on we see the 'dead' Bottom leap to his feet to interrupt the conversation between Demetrius and Theseus, which has much the same effect. The language which the workmen use in their play is a poor attempt at what they think is the 'correct' dramatic language of poetry. Their poetry has in fact more in common with doggerel, but notice how they abandon this 'inflated speech' when they speak directly to the audience in their more normal prose. The court make their sniping comments in prose, which is appropriate given that they are speaking about 'lower' or 'common' things. None the less, having the workmen speak poetry, of whatever quality, whilst the court speak prose, however wittily, is another example of how 'normal' patterns of behaviour are turned upside-down throughout *A Midsummer Night's Dream*.

| | |
|---|---|
| 75/0 | Workmen |
| 78/83 | Discord |
| 78/81 | Love |

---

**81  5 1 346  'No epilogue, I pray you; . . .'**
Theseus asks the workmen to omit the epilogue and dance instead. No doubt by now both he and the court have been amused enough and feel that they can bear no more of the workmen's absurd play.

There is an interesting dramatic parallel here, in the way dancing is used in the

| | |
|---|---|
| 77/82 | Theseus |
| 80/83 | Love |
| 64/82 | Music |
| 73/82 | Order |

## 54  Act 5

drama. The last dance we witnessed also came at the end of a piece of make-believe, when Titania and Oberon danced after the lovers had emerged from their exhausting ordeal in the wood. Then, as here, a dance is used to suggest an atmosphere of harmony and peace. Shakespeare's use of dance and music in *A Midsummer Night's Dream* is interesting and you should look out for other examples and try to work out why they appear where they do in the play and what dramatic use they are being put to.

---

**82  5 1 353  'The iron tongue of midnight . . .'**
Theseus announces that the ringing of the bell tells them that it is time for bed. This speech marks the last appearance of the human characters in the play and in it Theseus strengthens the feeling of human harmony, happiness and fulfilment. This is very different to the start of the play, which was marked by dispute, disharmony and strife. Because of this difference of atmosphere, Theseus's comment that it is 'almost fairy time' does not produce uneasiness in us. We do not feel concerned that the reappearance of the spirits will be the start of new ordeals for the human characters in the play. This feeling has been carefully produced by Shakespeare by his use of dance and language to suggest harmony, his use of humour in the playing of *Pyramus and Thisbe* and the development of the story to the point where we feel confident that all must now turn out well. Puck prepared us for this as long ago as the end of Act Three, when he told us that 'Jack shall have Jill;/Naught shall go ill'.

| 81/0 | Theseus |
| 81/84 | Music |
| 81/83 | Order |

---

**83  5 1 359  'A fortnight hold we . . .'**
Theseus says that their marriages – what he calls their 'new jollity' – shall be celebrated for a fortnight. Throughout *A Midsummer Night's Dream* we see that marriage is shown as the proper and most fulfilling outcome of mature true love. Women who are forced to endure virginity are depicted as unfulfilled, sad, lonely and unnatural. Any breakdown between relationships between two lovers is seen as unnatural and leading to nightmarish situations. Hermia actually wakens from a nightmare about a snake when she becomes separated from Lysander. Titania undergoes a humiliating nightmare as a result of the rift between her and Oberon and the wall in *Pyramus and Thisbe* is condemned as a 'vile' thing because it keeps two lovers apart.

| 80/0 | Discord |
| 78/85 | Illusion |
| 81/86 | Love |
| 82/84 | Order |

Another thing to be aware of here is the hidden message about Elizabethan society. *A Midsummer Night's Dream* takes the audience through discord to harmony. To the Elizabethans the maintenance of harmony within the world, especially within the political world of man, was vitally important. Shakespeare's play emphasizes the importance of harmony. The complicated jigsaw nature of the story of the play would have greatly entertained its contemporary audience, for the Elizabethans loved things with secret or hidden meanings, hence their general fascination with puns, poetry and language.

---

**84  5 1 361  'Now the hungry lion roars'**
Now that the human characters have departed for the last time, Puck enters to remind us that the world of the fairies is that of nature. It is a world of kindness towards humans, where the happiness of humans is the fairies' prime responsibility. It is this world which has come to the palace of Theseus and, in speeches rich with rhyming couplets, Puck, Oberon and Titania chant a magic spell of protection over it. Dancing and singing are used to reinforce this sense of harmony and emphasize the atmosphere of ritual.

| 67/85 | Oberon |
| 61/86 | Puck |
| 63/0 | Titania |
| 82/0 | Music |
| 75/86 | Mythology |
| 70/0 | Nature |
| 83/86 | Order |

---

**85  5 1 381  'Through the house give . . .'**
Oberon commands the fairy spirits to spread throughout the house to afford magical protection to the humans. The identification of supernatural creatures from the spirit world with moonlight is again strengthened by the

| 84/86 | Oberon |
| 77/86 | Darkness |
| 83/86 | Illusion |

use of the word 'glimmering', which suggests a flickering light, hovering in uncertainty between the world of reality and the world of the imaginary.

| | |
|---|---|
| 77/0 | Imagination |
| 70/0 | Moon |

## 86  5 1 413  'If we shadows have offended,'

Puck talks about the possibility that the 'shadows' have offended. There are several possible interpretations which suggest themselves here. For example, how far do you think Oberon has been justified in interfering in the lives of the humans in the play? Do you see him most accurately as a meddling nuisance who interferes in the lives of others for his own amusement? How much could we sympathize with any of the four young lovers if they discovered what Oberon had done and became angry with him about it?

| | |
|---|---|
| 85/0 | Oberon |
| 84/0 | Puck |
| 85/0 | Darkness |
| 85/0 | Illusion |
| 83/0 | Love |
| 84/0 | Mythology |
| 84/0 | Order |

Puck steps forward to talk directly to the audience, to beg their pardon if the play has offended anyone and to remind the audience that it is only make-believe. You should notice that this is not the first time this kind of thing has happened in the play, because the workmen did much the same when they performed *Pyramus and Thisbe* for the Duke. This repeating of a dramatic device in a slightly different context is used by Shakespeare to 'reflect' or 'echo' one part of the play from another and contributes to the play's interest and sense of structure.

Puck's reference to the cast of the play as 'shadows', a word Theseus also uses around line 208, is one of the many examples of the skilful use of language in this play. The play is about dreams and reality, about what is rational and what is irrational, about how hard it sometimes is to tell one from the other. Characters in the play are constantly hiding from each other and in some ways hiding from themselves. Much of the play is concerned with people discovering who they really love and who they really are. We find characters who are sometimes not what they appear to be (the ass-headed Bottom; the lovers), characters who are sometimes invisible to others (Oberon; the fairies), characters who are playing a part (the workmen; the cast of *A Midsummer Night's Dream*), and characters whose perceptions of reality are at times distorted by passion or by magic. Puck's comment that the play is populated by 'shadows' would fit all of these. An important question which *A Midsummer Night's Dream* raises for us is whether the world of 'shadows' – the world of the imagination – is more truly 'real' for people than the waking world of everyday experience.

Additionally, you should remember the way actual darkness and night are used in the play to suggest confusion, lack of mental clarity, mystery, fear and the 'darker' supernatural forces in man's mind. Finally, we might also notice that the play ends with the coming of night in this final scene and remember that as Elizabethan drama was often played outdoors dusk may indeed have actually been approaching the playhouse. Just as the sound of Theseus's hunting horns awoke the lovers from a time of illusions and dreams, so the applause of the theatre audience will break the magic spell which Shakespeare has woven and will mark an end to this journey through the imagination and a return from the land of illusion.

# Characters in the play

## Egeus

Egeus appears as a rather narrow-minded and fussy man. He is rather unimaginative and is the oldest of the human characters in the play.

At the start of the play Egeus has determined that his daughter Hermia will marry Demetrius. When she refuses he brings her before Theseus, the Duke of Athens, for trial. Egeus demands the full penalty of the law and seems not to have much sympathy for young love. When, at the end of the play, the four young lovers are discovered asleep together on the forest floor, Egeus wants the law to punish Lysander. Theseus overrules this request so that Hermia can marry the man she loves.

The contrast between Egeus and Theseus shows us the more sensitive and understanding behaviour of the more noble of the two men. This is complemented in the rest of the play by the way other groups of characters are portrayed as 'types', such as the workmen. Egeus, like many other characters in the play, is not well developed as an 'individual' and he may appear to us as rather shallow if looked at in this way. You will gain more from this particular play if you try to look at the characters, the settings and the story as representing 'types', ideas and standard moral dilemmas from Elizabethan society. As many of these things have persisted without too much change into modern times you should have little difficulty recognizing most of these dramatic conventions.

## The Fairies

### Oberon

Oberon is the most powerful and influential figure in his world, just as Theseus is in the human world. But whilst Theseus shows responsibility and insight, Oberon displays a more impetuous and changing nature. In this respect he is similar to Puck. Theirs is a world which is a mixture of supernatural beauty and almost juvenile pranks. It is not without significance that Oberon's power and influence are the most strongly felt of any in *A Midsummer Night's Dream*.

Our first encounter with Oberon shows him to be jealous, in that he wants the Indian boy from Titania. He is a powerful and elemental force, supernatural and mysterious, but one which does have some pity for the situations of humans. He is clearly used to getting his own way and is angry, even vindictive, when thwarted, even when this is by his wife, although we might feel that if Titania is giving a great deal of her time to the Indian boy the problem may be that she has not been paying enough attention to her husband. Oberon may regard this as disloyalty.

Oberon is a force of magic and profound natural beauty, but he wants to use his power to humiliate Titania when he cannot have what he wants. His language is, like that of the other fairies, a mixture of goodness and mischievousness and it is this combination of the force of magic and the power of language which best reflects his character.

He is able to see things which are hidden even from his right-hand sprite, Puck, and has a wide knowledge of the force of plants and herbs. Indeed, Oberon's descriptions of the power of the love juice, the sea, mermaids' music, the night and the beauty of nature reinforces our understanding that he is supernaturally at one with all these elemental forces.

Oberon's realm is far removed from the common sense world of Theseus and this is powerfully reflected in the language which he uses. The world of Oberon is one of dreams and irrationality, filled with the power of the imagination. So Oberon too is a dream figure – he has influence over the world of humans but is not bound by it.

## Titania

Titania is characterized throughout the play as wonderfully magical and gloriously beautiful. She lives in a world of sensuousness and her relationship with Bottom is easily the most intimate in the play. Her character is more sensuous and physical than Oberon's and the power of her language vividly evokes the beauty of the world in which the fairies live. However, she also shows considerable strength of character and will not submit willingly to Oberon over the Indian boy.

Titania's entanglement with Bottom is both entrancing and comic, yet has the effect of being even more ridiculous than her adoration for the Indian boy. The relationship is both innocent and intimate; her light and delicate character contrasts well with Bottom's 'mortal grossness'. Much of the effect created is achieved by the language of Titania, whose speeches abound with evocative pictures of the beauty and delight of her world and their overwhelming sense of richness and fertility.

As with the four young human lovers, the relationship of Oberon and Titania is improved by their period of disaffection. A renewal of their love brings greater happiness to all of them.

Puck: *'The wisest aunt telling the saddest tale sometime for three-foot stool mistaketh me.'*

## Puck

To the audiences of Shakespeare's day Puck, or Robin Goodfellow as he was sometimes known, was a folklore figure whom many believed in. He has almost none of the dignity and grandeur of Oberon or Titania and specializes instead in making mischief, something at which he is expert. He moves between the world of the fairies and the humans in order to play pranks on the latter, although he is not altogether reliable when it comes to following instructions. When he becomes involved in something he never gets emotionally entangled, unlike every other character in the play, but his involvement stems only from a desire to stir up another situation to mock. He provides most of the situations which generate the ludicrous and irresponsible feelings which run through the play.

Puck upsets people with great enthusiasm and the audience find this engaging and amusing. He represents the love of practical jokes which many people have, but in his case it is uncomplicated by feelings of remorse or restraint. However, his detached and almost unemotional manner makes him difficult for audiences to really like. Often we feel that Puck's laughter is hard to share because it is devoid of that human sympathy which provokes much of mankind's humour at itself.

Puck is a loyal servant of Oberon whose errors are caused by misinterpretation or literal mindedness rather than disobedience. Much of the resulting comedy is therefore of a farcical nature.

Puck is, in essence, an ambiguous figure in that he is irresponsible but, because he is controlled by Oberon, acts for the useful purpose of serving the mortals and helping to bring them eventual happiness.

## *Hippolyta*

In Greek legend Hippolyta was the Queen of the Amazons who was ravished by Theseus and defeated by him in battle. In the legend Hippolyta flees from Theseus after their battle and dies of grief, but in Shakespeare's drama they are lovers and she is to marry him. She provides the image of mature love which forms a contrast to the impulsive love of the four young lovers.

Hippolyta displays both human warmth and insight and it is she who, at the end of the play, realizes that the lovers' experience in the wood may be more than just a figment of their imaginations. Although the workmen's play amuses her by its amateurishness, we should notice that her amusement is more kindly than that of many of the rest of the court.

## *The Lovers*

These four young lovers should be thought of both as individual characters in the play and as a quartet. Each of them has unique characteristics, but they also have a great deal in common, and this is one reason why they are sometimes confused with each other.

This ambiguity is deliberate because the quartet represents the theme of young love as well as four individuals. Some critics have found the four members of the quartet completely 'characterless', but have felt that this was appropriate in the play, because they are meant to be symbols rather than dramatic characters. Others have argued that the young lovers have not been well created by Shakespeare and are virtually interchangeable because of their lack of individuality. You should think about how far you feel able to agree with either of these views. What evidence from the play could you point to which might support or refute either of them?

Like many other young lovers, these four characters share extremes of passion which run from tenderness to cruelty. Their language is often very refined in the rather artificial style of the day, although Shakespeare cleverly writes in such a way that we often find this amusing, as we do their passions. Demetrius's vows of love to Helena are spoken with such passionate seriousness that they become comic, especially as we know that because of the love juice his feelings are only an illusion.

When the young men break off with the women for whom they have previously declared their love, we see a rather callous and brutal side to them, which might make us wonder to what extent they are immature underneath their sophisticated, gentlemanly gloss. Helena and Hermia also use language which veers from the subtle to the contemptuous, as when they confront each other in Act Three. This mixture of the language of tenderness with mercurial temper, of callous bluntness with ornamental delicacy, is portrayed by Shakespeare as typical of youth's inability to see the ludicrous side of being in love. The quartet represent the traditional image of young lovers as found in much of the literature of Shakespeare's day, and this is why they often speak in the artificial way that a contemporary audience would have expected them to speak, except when they are falling out when they become amusing and speak in a more common way.

## *Demetrius*

If anything, Demetrius is even more callous at times than Lysander and it is likely that the audience will not feel much sympathy for him. We see this at the start of the play, when he throws over Helena for Hermia and we might conclude that he is a young man of fickle temperament. His meeting with Helena in the wood, before the love juice has been put on his eyes, would probably confirm this view of him. It is important to remember that at the end of the play he is the only character with love juice still on his eyes, and therefore his feelings for Helena are attributable more to that than to his own desires. Only the fact that this illusion brings about a happy conclusion might make this situation acceptable to the audience.

Although at the end of the drama we might feel that Helena deserves to be loved by Demetrius – after all she has loved him steadfastly throughout the play – we should also think about how right, moral or fair the situation is. Has Oberon, with his magic juice, forced Demetrius to love someone against his will? How should we feel about this? And is Helena the victim of a rather cruel joke by Oberon if she thinks that Demetrius actually loves her? Think carefully about whether it really matters which way these questions are answered, or whether it is the case that in life a happy illusion is sometimes preferable to an unhappy truth.

## *Helena*

We learn early on in the play that Helena was once loved by Demetrius but that he deserted her for Hermia. So at the beginning of the play we see Helena as a beautiful young woman who is unhappy and rejected. She knows that her love is no longer returned by Demetrius and that her doting on him is rather unhealthy and undignified, but she cannot help herself because her emotions are too strong. Her efforts to regain the love of Demetrius are touching and audiences often feel very sympathetic towards her because of this.

Helena is distinguished from Hermia physically by being taller than her but more timid. Emotionally they are different in so far as Helena has to suffer much more than Hermia before she finds happiness at the end of the play. Also, Helena's lover is bound to her at the end of the play only by an illusion – it is only because of the love juice which is still on Demetrius's eyes that he loves her. Helena is therefore a sadder figure throughout the play, and even her final happiness is founded upon a kind of deceit.

Helena's name, which comes from the Greek for 'light', reminds us of Helen of Troy, which is probably a reference to her fair beauty. There are also other interesting allusions to mythology. In the Greek myths Helen is carried off by Theseus when she is a child, but her brothers rescue her. When Helen later marries she has a child called Hermione, whose name is very close to that of Hermia in Shakespeare's play.

## *Hermia*

Hermia's name contains strong echoes of the Greek Hermes, who was the messenger of the gods. In Roman mythology this was Mercury, who was noted for a fiery personality, as witnessed by the character of Mercutio in *Romeo and Juliet*. We see that in *A Midsummer Night's Dream* Hermia also has a fiery streak in her.

She is, in her father's eyes, stubborn and wilful, although we may see her instead as determined and loyal. She runs away with her lover Lysander so that they can be together where the laws of Athens cannot reach them. Her deliberate disobedience of her father in this way would have reflected very badly on her in Shakespeare's time, when obedience to one's parents was seen as most important.

Although Hermia is brave and strong we still find the bizarre problems she faces in the wood amusing, even though she clearly does not. Certainly her row with her old school-friend Helena is amusing, especially when their argument degenerates to the level of the farcical references to the fact that Hermia is shorter than Helena.

The audience is likely to be sympathetic towards Hermia; she has a domineering father but she shows great character in her defiance of him. She also reveals a modest and 'proper' side to her nature when she insists in the wood that Lysander sleep apart from her. At the end of the play we tend to feel pleased therefore that Hermia is married to Lysander, whom she has loved all along, rather than to Demetrius, as her father wished.

## *Lysander*

Lysander is the most outspoken of the four lovers and he plans to run away with Hermia in defiance of Egeus, who sees Lysander as deceitful. The plan seems very romantic, especially when we consider that he has also stolen Hermia's love away from Demetrius, Egeus's favoured bridegroom. Just as the audience is likely to have little sympathy with Demetrius at the start of the play, so it is likely to regard Lysander in a good light because of the way he behaves.

Lysander's contemptuous rejection of Hermia in the wood, although due to the love juice on his eyes, therefore seems especially callous and shocking. The incident highlights the fickle and ridiculous nature of love, although at the end of the play all is made well again when Theseus overrules Egeus and allows the two lovers to marry.

## Theseus

As the ruler of Athens, Theseus is approached at the start of the play by Egeus, who wants the law to support him in making his daughter marry who her father wishes. We see from the way that Theseus handles the affair that he is a firm but kindly man who displays wisdom and maturity in setting a four day 'cooling-off' period for tempers to calm. Theseus obviously takes his position in society seriously and has a genuine interest in the welfare of all his subjects. This is why he takes Egeus aside for some private words of advice and why, at the end of the play, he overrules Egeus and allows Hermia to marry the man she loves rather than the one her father chose for her. This is important because in doing this Theseus puts aside the laws of Athens for a higher cause – that of love. This demonstrates that whilst he can be firm about enforcing the law, as in the play's opening scene, he can be swift to set it aside when it runs counter to common sense and the wishes of the four lovers. Doubtless his own affections for Hippolyta make him particularly sensitive to the lovers' feelings.

Theseus's kindness is also shown by his reaction to the play performed by the workmen. Although he finds their rather bungled attempt amusing, his humour is not without kindness and he takes their gift to him in the spirit in which it is given. Theseus has all the characteristics of a good Elizabethan ruler, he is benevolent, conscious of his responsibilities as well as of his powers, is a patron of the arts and an active sportsman.

Theseus is highly regarded by Titania, a regard which links him with the spirit world within the wood, and at the end of the play the fairy spirits all join in wishing happiness to Theseus and his bride.

Snout: *'In this same interlude it doth befall
That I – one Snout by name – present a wall.'*

## The Workmen: Bottom, Flute, Quince, Snout, Snug, Starveling

Bottom the weaver is the most well-developed dramatic character amongst the Athenian workmen. He is also the most wildly enthusiastic and self-confident! By his various adventures he connects the world of the workmen with that of the aristocrats and the fairies.

## Characters in the play

Throughout the play we see Bottom as a plain, honest and simple man, as is well illustrated by his charming conversation with Titania's four small fairy attendants. His innocence is made all the more noticeable in such sensuous surroundings. His name, like that of his fellow workmen, is connected with his trade, being the name of the spool around which a weaver winds a skein of thread; it is also, considering the love scene with Titania and his appearance there, a pun, or joke, on 'ass'.

Much of the language in the scenes where Bottom is in the world of the fairies is very beautiful, and he is surrounded by a complicated mixture of emotions which range from the comic to the sensuous, from the innocent to the moving.

It is typical of Bottom that he cannot distinguish between dream and reality, either when he awakens from Titania's arms within the wood, or when it comes to realizing that the workmen's play is a deliberate illusion and will be recognized as such by its audience. In this, Bottom's confusion sums up the spirit of *A Midsummer Night's Dream* perfectly – we can be delighted by the theatrical illusion and believe it to be true, within the magic of the drama and whilst we are watching the play, but we know that the events are not really true.

It is ironic that Bottom himself can believe in one sort of imaginative reality – of fairies – but not the other – the play in which he is an actor. It is also ironic that it should be the ass-headed Bottom who is given the most poetic experience of any of the play's characters when the most alluring and magical woman in the play falls in love with him, for it is Bottom who bungles the poetry of *Pyramus and Thisbe* most completely. Bottom does have a gift for language however; his constant misuse of long words is to some extent a sign of his ignorance, whilst the limited vocabulary of the rest of the workmen accurately reveals limitations in their education. Bottom may fail miserably in his role at the centre of the workmen's play, but he is chosen to play a central part in the greatest illusion in Shakespeare's play. The way his language constantly tries to escape the everyday world of the workman and reach out towards the poetic is a reflection of his special role. His comment that 'reason and love keep little company nowadays' is a truth which the educated and sophisticated courtiers do not perceive.

Whilst Bottom is an important character, the other workmen have an important role to play also, although theirs is more of a collective effort and we can consider them more as a group. The workmen are in some ways rather like the young lovers, because as well as being individual characters they also represent between them a theme. Appropriately, the workmen are less well drawn than the lovers because they represent the clumsy sincerity of the naïve common people. Like Theseus and his court we in the audience can laugh at their unsophisticated attempts to put on a dramatic work of art, but we should also recognize that our feelings towards them are complicated. The workmen's attempts to create noble feelings may be ludicrous but their simple, literal-minded honesty is also deeply touching.

Flute is a bellows-mender who has to play the woman's part of Thisbe in the workmen's play, about which he is unhappy. Peter Quince is the director who has a rather hard time keeping his cast in order, especially the enthusiastic Bottom, but he is practical and determined. We see his attempts to stage the play as well meaning but ridiculous. Snout, the tinker, has the honour of being 'Wall' in the workmen's play and much of the amusement this generates stems from this ridiculous situation. Snug, the joiner, has trouble learning lines on account of his self-confessed slow wits. He is told that he may do his lion roaring 'extempore' – that is, he may improvise it rather than learn it from a script! Starveling, like Bottom, loses patience with the courtiers, in his case when they laugh at his portrayal of Moonshine. He interrupts his performance to speak directly to the audience.

Most of the character names in the play are Greek, which fit in well with the setting of Athens. The workmen's names are an exception to this, being extremely English. The only other exceptions are the names of Titania's fairies, Peasblossom, Moth, Cobweb and Mustardseed, which are drawn from nature. Quince and Snug are both carpenters as their names indicate, for 'quince', or 'quines' as they were sometimes called, were names for blocks of wood, and any joiner would be expected to put them together 'snugly'. Flute would mend bellows and also fix church organs which whistled when damaged or out of tune; the actor playing him may well have adopted a thin and piping voice on this account. Tailors seems to have been commonly regarded as thin people, and Robin Starveling's name conjures up a thin, bird-like figure. As a tinker, Snout would have spent a lot of his time mending the spouts (snouts) on pans and other vessels.

# What happens in each act

## Act One

### Scene 1
The play begins with Theseus, the Duke of Athens, and Hippolyta looking forward to their wedding in four day's time. Hippolyta is the Queen of the Amazons, over whom Theseus has just won a victory in battle. Theseus orders celebrations to be organized to pass the time until the wedding. At this point Egeus arrives with a problem which has infuriated him. He has promised that his daughter, Hermia, will marry a young man called Demetrius. Unfortunately for Egeus, his daughter is in love with another young man, Lysander. Theseus explains to Hermia that an old law of Athens states that she must marry the man her father has chosen or else face death. Her only other alternative is to spend the rest of her life in a nunnery, shut away from men. Theseus gives her until the day of his own wedding to make up her mind which she will choose to do.

As soon as they are left alone Lysander and Hermia agree to run away and live with his aunt, where they can be married. They arrange to meet the following night in the woods outside Athens.

Helena arrives at this point. She is a girl who Demetrius wooed before Hermia and she makes it plain that she is still in love with him. Lysander and Hermia try to encourage Helena by telling her about their plans to elope, pointing out that this will mean that Helena will have Demetrius all to herself.

Helena is left alone and complains bitterly about the unfairness of love. She decides to tell Demetrius about the elopement plans of Lysander and Hermia in a bid to win back his love.

Bottom: 'A very good piece of work, I assure you, and a merry.'

### Scene 2
A group of workmen from Athens arrive to rehearse a play which they hope the Duke will ask them to perform at his wedding. They have come outside the city so that they can rehearse in secret and keep the subject of their play a surprise. Although Quince, the carpenter, seems to be the director of the play it is Bottom, the weaver, who wants to take charge and even offers to play all the parts himself!

*What happens in each act*

Quince tells everyone that the play is about Pyramus and Thisbe. This famous story of thwarted love was from classical literature and would have been well known to many people in Shakespeare's audience. Bottom is eventually persuaded that he is to play only one character, that of Pyramus.

## Act Two

### Scene 1

Oberon, King of the Spirits, and his Queen, Titania, are having a quarrel about which of them should have as a servant a boy who has been stolen from an Indian king. Oberon's servant, Puck, explains to us how the quarrel arose and also describes how powerful an influence the spirit world has over humans when they stray into the forest. Puck boasts about the mischievous way he uses his own power.

Oberon and Titania enter and begin to quarrel. Titania refuses to give Oberon the boy. In his anger, Oberon orders Puck to find a special flower whose juice has magical power. Oberon intends to squeeze the juice of this flower onto Titania's eyes whilst she is asleep. The juice will make Titania fall in love with the first living thing that she sees upon awakening. In this way Oberon hopes to humiliate Titania and make her give him the boy. Oberon knows of an antidote to the juice and intends to both revenge and amuse himself with this power.

At this point Demetrius arrives followed by Helen, who has told him about the elopement plans of Hermia and Lysander. Demetrius is searching for Hermia and Lysander in the wood, because he wants to keep Hermia for himself. He says he is being driven mad because he cannot find Hermia and cruelly tells Helena to go away because he hates her. Helena says she cannot leave him and will follow him like a dog. He runs off, leaving her to the wild beasts, and in desperation she chases after him. Oberon is invisible to humans and has therefore been able to listen to their conversation without them knowing. He says he will turn the tables on the two by making Demetrius love Helena.

Puck returns and Oberon tells him that half of the love juice is for Titania and the other half is now for Demetrius; Puck will recognize Demetrius because he is wearing Athenian clothes. Oberon does not realize that there is another young Athenian in the woods – Lysander – or that Puck will get the two mixed up.

### Scene 2

Titania enters, surrounded by her attendants who sing her to sleep. Oberon appears, squeezes the love juice onto her eyes and then departs.

Lysander and Hermia enter; they have met up in the woods as arranged but have now become lost. They are tired and lie down to sleep, although Hermia, out of modesty, makes Lysander sleep some way from her. After they fall asleep Puck enters, looking for the Athenian man as Oberon instructed him. Puck sees Lysander asleep on the ground and, mistaking him for Demetrius, squeezes love juice onto his eyes. As Puck leaves to report to Oberon, Demetrius enters, still being followed by Helena. Demetrius runs off, leaving Helena.

Helena does not notice Hermia but sees Lysander asleep on the ground. She wakens him and he promptly falls in love with her because of the love juice on his eyes. She becomes convinced that he is making fun of her and runs away, upset. Lysander rushes after her, leaving Hermia alone. When Hermia awakens she becomes frightened at being alone in the forest and runs off in search of Lysander.

## Act Three

### Scene 1

Bottom and his friends enter the same clearing which featured in the last scene. They do not notice Titania asleep and begin their rehearsal by discussing the problems they foresee with their play *Pyramus and Thisbe*. Bottom is worried that when Pyramus draws his sword to kill himself this will frighten the ladies. Snout is concerned that the lion, played by Snug, will also frighten the ladies. They arrange for a prologue to be spoken to tell the ladies not to be frightened and for Snug's face to be visible through the lion costume. Quince has been wondering about two other problems – how to show the scene in which Pyramus and Thisbe meet by moonlight, and the one where they speak to each other through a wall. These problems are solved by having one of the workmen with a lantern pretend to be the moon whilst another, covered in sand, clay, plaster and small stones, pretends to be a wall. As the workmen now think that they have solved all the problems of production they begin to rehearse. At this point Puck enters and decides to watch in case he sees an opportunity to create mischief.

The rehearsal goes ahead with the workmen making several ridiculous mistakes. At one point in the muddle, Bottom forgets his cue and has to be called on stage by Quince. As Bottom enters we see that he has on the head of an ass and we realize that this is a piece of Puck's mischief. Bottom does not understand why all his friends rush away in terror. He does not know that Puck is also adding to the confusion by appearing to the workmen in various frightening forms and making them scratch themselves on bushes and briars as they run off. When Snout and Quince briefly reappear to tell Bottom about his changed appearance he suspects that the episode is a trick by his friends who are trying to make him look foolish. To show that he is not frightened by their prank, Bottom decides to sing a song.

The noise awakens Titania who, because of the love juice, falls in love with him as soon as she sees him. They go to Titania's bower, attended by her fairies.

**Scene 2**
Oberon is wondering how the love juice is working with Titania and whether she has woken up yet. Puck enters and tells Oberon about the workmen's play, the ass's head on Bottom and Titania's love for the monster. Oberon is delighted and asks Puck about the other Athenian. Puck reports that he has accomplished this task also.

At this point Demetrius and Hermia enter and Puck's mistake becomes clear – he has put love juice onto the eyes of the wrong young man. Hermia runs away from the love-struck Demetrius and he, exhausted by the pursuit, falls asleep. Oberon tells Puck to go and get Helena so that he can reunite her with Demetrius and, whilst Puck does this, Oberon squeezes love juice onto the eyes of Demetrius.

Puck returns, followed by Helena. Lysander arrives and, still under the influence of the love juice, begs Helena to love him. The noise wakes Demetrius and, because he too has love juice on his eyes, he sees Helena and falls in love with her. Helena now has not only Lysander chasing her, but also has to contend with the professed love of Demetrius, who so recently scorned her. Helena thinks that the two men are mocking her and that this is a trick.

Hermia returns and is pleased to find that Lysander is safe, although she is confused when he tells her that he now loves Helena. The two men begin quarrelling about who loves whom and make fools of themselves because they are acting under the influence of the love juice. Helena concludes that not only have the two men acted together to ridicule her, but that Hermia is part of the cruel jest also. The two women begin quarrelling about which of them is scorning the other. Lysander challenges Demetrius to a duel in order to settle matters and the two men leave. Helena runs away, followed by Hermia.

Oberon is concerned at the confusion which has resulted from Puck's actions with the love juice. Puck is much entertained, but Oberon, who is benevolent towards humans, realizes that the duel between Lysander and Demetrius will not be a joke. Oberon tells Puck to make all well between the humans whilst he goes to beg the Indian boy from Titania and release her from her illusory love for Bottom so that 'all things shall be peace'.

Puck causes the four human lovers to become hopelessly lost, confused and exhausted so that they fall asleep on the forest floor. He then squeezes the antidote to the love juice on the eyes of Lysander but not, we notice, on the eyes of Demetrius.

Lysander: *'Nothing truer – 'tis no jest
That I do hate thee and love Helena.'*

## Act Four

### Scene 1

The four human lovers remain asleep. Titania is still in love with Bottom, who is pampered by her attendant fairies. He is offered food and music and both he and Titania eventually fall asleep. Oberon is now satisfied that he has humiliated his Queen enough and he explains to Puck that Titania was so in love with Bottom that she even agreed to give him the Indian boy in return for being left alone. Now that he has everything that he wants, Oberon begins to pity Titania and squeezes the antidote to the love juice on her eyes. When she awakens she is appalled at the sight of the creature she has loved. Puck is ordered to remove the ass's head from Bottom. Oberon, Titania and the fairies all leave the stage as dawn breaks and hunting horns are heard approaching.

The hunting horns and the baying of dogs herald the arrival of Theseus and Hippolyta on the day of their wedding. Theseus orders his huntsmen to awaken the four lovers with the sound of their horns. We see that Demetrius now loves Helena, whilst Lysander loves Hermia. Egeus (Hermia's father) wants the law to be kept and Hermia therefore sentenced for disobeying him – we remember that at the start of the play Egeus had decided that Hermia was to marry Demetrius. But Theseus overrules Egeus and says that the four lovers shall be married as they wish, at the same time as he and Hippolyta are wed. They all leave the stage to make preparations.

Bottom, who has remained unnoticed, wakes up and still thinks that he is in the middle of the rehearsal of the play. He is surprised that the other actors are not there and as he wakens fully, begins to recall his fantastic experiences. Bottom's memories seem to him like a wonderful dream and he decides to get Peter Quince to write a ballad about them.

### Scene 2

The workmen are depressed because they cannot find Bottom. Snug enters to tell them that the Duke and some other lords and ladies have been married. This depresses them further, for it means that the time for their play to be performed is now very close. Bottom suddenly appears and starts organizing everybody, as theirs is the play which has been 'preferred'. They all leave for the palace.

## Act Five

### Scene 1

The four young lovers have been telling Theseus and Hippolyta about their magical experiences in the wood. Theseus feels that love has inflamed their imaginations and led them into delusions, but Hippolyta senses that there is something more to it than that, although she is unable to say what. The young newlyweds enter and Theseus decides that of all the entertainment on offer, *Pyramus and Thisbe* sounds the most amusing. The court expect the play to be funny because it will be performed by humble workmen who have no experience of acting at all. The play goes ahead, with the court making continuous comments amidst all the workmen's mistakes. The performance is concluded with a dance, a bell sounds, and the humans leave the stage.

Puck enters, followed by Oberon, Titania and the fairies. Oberon blesses the marriages of the humans. Puck addresses the theatre audience to suggest to them that the whole play may have been a dream, and to ask for their applause for the actors.

Bottom: *For the short and the long is, our play is preferred.*

# Coursework and preparing for the examination

If you wish to gain a certificate in English literature then there is no substitute for studying the text/s on which you are to be examined. If you cannot be bothered to do that, then neither this guide nor any other will be of use to you.

Here we give advice on studying the text, writing a good essay, producing coursework, and sitting the examination. However, if you meet problems you should ask your teacher for help.

## Studying the text

**No, not just read–study.** You must read your text at least twice. Do not dismiss it if you find a first reading difficult or uninteresting. Approach the text with an open mind and you will often find a second reading more enjoyable. When you become a more experienced reader enjoyment usually follows from a close study of the text, when you begin to appreciate both what the author is saying and the skill with which it is said.

Having read the text, you must now study it. We restrict our remarks here to novels and plays, though much of what is said can also be applied to poetry.

1 You will know in full detail all the major incidents in your text, **why**, **where** and **when** they happen, **who** is involved, **what** leads up to them and what follows.

2 You must show that you have an **understanding of the story**, the **characters**, and the **main ideas** which the author is exploring.

3 In a play you must know what happens in each act, and more specifically the organization of the scene structure–how one follows from and builds upon another. Dialogue in both plays and novels is crucial. You must have a detailed knowledge of the major dialogues and soliloquies and the part they play in the development of plot, and the development and drawing of character.

4 When you write about a novel you will not normally be expected to quote or to refer to specific lines but references to incidents and characters must be given, and they must be accurate and specific.

5 In writing about a play you will be expected both to paraphrase dialogue and quote specific lines, always provided, of course, that they are actually contributing something to your essay!

To gain full marks in coursework and/or in an examination you will also be expected to show your own reaction to, and appreciation of, the text studied. The teacher or examiner always welcomes those essays which demonstrate the student's own thoughtful response to the text. Indeed, questions often specify such a requirement, so do participate in those classroom discussions, the debates, class dramatizations of all or selected parts of your text, and the many other activities which enable a class to share and grow in their understanding and feeling for literature.

**Making notes**
A half-hearted reading of your text, or watching the 'film of the book' will not give you the necessary knowledge to meet the above demands.

As you study the text jot down sequences of events; quotations of note; which events precede and follow the part you are studying; the characters involved; what the part being studied contributes to the plot and your understanding of character and ideas.

Write single words, phrases and short sentences which can be quickly reviewed and which will help you to gain a clear picture of the incident being studied. Make your notes neat and orderly, with headings to indicate chapter, scene, page, incident, character, etc, so that you can quickly find the relevant notes or part of the text when revising.

## Writing the essay

Good essays are like good books, in miniature; they are thought about, planned, logically structured, paragraphed, have a clearly defined pattern and development of thought, and are presented clearly–and with neat writing! All of this will be to no avail if the tools you use, i.e. words, and the skill with which you put them together to form your sentences and paragraphs are severely limited.

How good is your general and literary vocabulary? Do you understand and can you make appropriate use of such terms as 'soliloquy', 'character', 'plot', 'mood', 'dramatically effective', 'comedy', 'allusion', 'humour', 'imagery', 'irony', 'paradox', 'anti-climax', 'tragedy'? These are all words which examiners have commented on as being misunderstood by students.

Do you understand 'metaphor', 'simile', 'alliteration'? Can you say what their effect is on you, the reader, and how they enable the author to express himself more effectively than by the use of a different literary device? If you cannot, you are employing your time ineffectively by using them.

You are writing an English literature essay and your writing should be literate and appropriate. Slang, colloquialisms and careless use of words are not tolerated in such essays.

**Essays for coursework**
The exact number of essays you will have to produce and their length will vary; it depends upon the requirements of the examination board whose course you are following, and whether you will be judged solely on coursework or on a mixture of coursework and examination.

As a guide, however your course is structured, you will be required to provide a folder containing at least ten essays, and from that folder approximately five will be selected for moderation purposes. Of those essays, one will normally have been done in class-time under conditions similar to those of an examination. The essays must cover the complete range of course requirements and be the unaided work of the student. One board specifies that these pieces of continuous writing should be a minimum of 400 words long, and another, a minimum of 500 words long. Ensure that you know what is required for your course, and do not aim for the minimum amount–write a full essay then prune it down if necessary.

Do take care over the presentation of your final folder of coursework. There are many devices on the market which will enable you to bind your work neatly, and in such a way that you can easily insert new pieces. Include a 'Contents' page and a front and back cover to keep your work clean. Ring binders are unsuitable items to hand in for **final** assessment purposes as they are much too bulky.

What sort of coursework essays will you be set? All boards lay down criteria similar to the following for the range of student response to literature that the coursework must cover.

Work must demonstrate that the student:

1 shows an understanding not only of surface meaning but also of a deeper awareness of themes and attitudes;

2 recognizes and appreciates ways in which authors use language;

3 recognizes and appreciates ways in which writers achieve their effects, particularly in how the work is structured and in its characterization;

4 can write imaginatively in exploring and developing ideas so as to communicate a sensitive and informed personal response to what is read.

Much of what is said in the section **'Writing essays in an examination'** (below) is relevant here, but for coursework essays you have the advantage of plenty of time to prepare your work–so take advantage of it.

There is no substitute for arguing, discussing and talking about a question on a particular text or theme. Your teacher should give you plenty of opportunity for this in the classroom. Listening to what others say about a subject often opens up for you new ways to look at and respond to it. The same can be said for reading about a topic. Be careful not to copy down slavishly what others say and write. Jot down notes then go away and think about what you have heard, read and written. Make more notes of your own and then start to clarify your own thoughts, feelings and emotions on the subject about which you are writing. Most students make the mistake of doing their coursework essays in a rush–you have time so use it.

Take a great deal of care in planning your work. From all your notes, write a rough draft and then start the task of really perfecting it.

1 Look at your arrangement of paragraphs, is there a logical development of thought or argument? Do the paragraphs need rearranging in order? Does the first or last sentence of any paragraph need redrafting in order to provide a sensible link with the preceding or next paragraph?

2 Look at the pattern of sentences within each paragraph. Are your thoughts and ideas clearly developed and expressed? Have you used any quotations, paraphrases, or references to incidents to support your opinions and ideas? Are those references relevant and apt, or just 'padding'?

3 Look at the words you have used. Try to avoid repeating words in close proximity one to another. Are the words you have used to comment on the text being studied the most appropriate and effective, or just the first ones you thought of?

4 Check your spelling and punctuation.

5 Now write a final draft, the quality of which should reflect the above considerations.

### Writing essays in an examination

**Read the question.** Identify the key words and phrases. Write them down, and as they are dealt with in your essay plan, tick them off.

**Plan your essay.** Spend about five minutes jotting down ideas; organize your thoughts and ideas into a logical and developing order–a structure is essential to the production of a good essay. Remember, brief, essential notes only!

### Write your essay

**How long should it be?** There is no magic length. What you must do is answer the question set, fully and sensitively in the time allowed. You will probably have about forty minutes to answer an essay question, and within that time you should produce an essay between roughly 350 and 500 words in length. Very short answers will not do justice to the question, very long answers will probably contain much irrelevant information and waste time that should be spent on the next answer.

**How much quotation?** Use only that which is apt and contributes to the clarity and quality of your answer. No examiner will be impressed by 'padding'.

### What will the examiners be looking for in an essay?

1 An answer to the question set, and not a prepared answer to another, albeit slightly similar question done in class.

2 A well-planned, logically structured and paragraphed essay with a beginning, middle and end.

3 Accurate references to plot, character, theme, as required by the question.

4 Appropriate, brief, and if needed, frequent quotation and references to support and demonstrate the comments that you are making in your essay.

5 Evidence that reading the text has prompted in you a personal response to it, as well as some judgment and appreciation of its literary merit.

**How do you prepare to do this?**

1 During your course you should write between three to five essays on each text.

2 Make good use of class discussion etc, as mentioned in a previous paragraph on page 73.

3 Try to see a live performance of a play. It may help to see a film of a play or book, though be aware that directors sometimes leave out episodes, change their order, or worse, add episodes that are not in the original–so be very careful. In the end, there is no substitute for **reading and studying** the text!

Try the following exercises without referring to any notes or text.

1 Pick a character from your text.

2 Make a list of his/her qualities–both positive and negative ones, or aspects that you cannot quite define. Jot down single words to describe each quality. If you do not know the word you want, use a thesaurus, but use it in conjunction with a dictionary and make sure you are fully aware of the meaning of each word you use.

3 Write a short sentence which identifies one or more places in the text where you think each quality is demonstrated.

4 Jot down any brief quotation, paraphrase of conversation or outline of an incident which shows that quality.

5 Organize the list. Identify groupings which contrast the positive and negative aspects of character.

6 Write a description of that character which makes full use of the material you have just prepared.

7 What do you think of the character you have just described? How has he/she reacted to and coped with the pressures of the other characters, incidents, and the setting of the story? Has he/she changed in any way? In no more than 100 words, including 'evidence' taken from the text, write a balanced assessment of the character, and draw some conclusions.

You should be able to do the above without notes, and without the text, unless you are to take an examination which allows the use of plain texts. In plain text examinations you are allowed to take in a copy of your text. It must be without notes, either your own or the publisher's. The intention is to enable you to consult a text in the examination so as to confirm memory of detail, thus enabling a candidate to quote and refer more accurately in order to illustrate his/her views that more effectively. Examiners will expect a high standard of accurate reference, quotation and comment in a plain text examination.

## Sitting the examination

You will have typically between two and five essays to write and you will have roughly 40 minutes, on average, to write each essay.

On each book you have studied, you should have a choice of doing at least one out of two or three essay titles set.

1 **Before sitting the exam**, make sure you are completely clear in your mind that you know exactly how many questions you must answer, which sections of the paper you must tackle, and how many questions you may, or must, attempt on any one book or in any one section of the paper. If you are not sure, ask your teacher.

2 **Always read the instructions** given at the top of your examination paper. They are

there to help you. Take your time, and try to relax–panicking will not help.

3 **Be very clear about timing, and organizing your time.**

(a) Know how long the examination is.
(b) Know how many questions you must do.
(c) Divide (b) into (a) to work out how long you may spend on each question. (Bear in mind that some questions may attract more marks, and should therefore take proportionately more time.)
(d) Keep an eye on the time, and do not spend more than you have allowed for any one question.
(e) If you have spare time at the end you can come back to a question and do more work on it.
(f) Do not be afraid to jot down notes as an aid to memory, but do cross them out carefully after use–a single line will do!

4 **Do not rush the decision** as to which question you are going to answer on a particular text.

(a) Study each question carefully.
(b) Be absolutely sure what each one is asking for.
(c) Make your decision as to which you will answer.

5 **Having decided which question** you will attempt:

(a) jot down the key points of the actual question–use single words or short phrases;
(b) think about how you are going to arrange your answer. Five minutes here, with some notes jotted down will pay dividends later;
(c) write your essay, and keep an eye on the time!

6 **Adopt the same approach** for all questions. Do write answers for the maximum number of questions you are told to attempt. One left out will lose its proportion of the total marks. Remember also, you will never be awarded extra marks, over and above those already allocated, if you write an extra long essay on a particular question.

7 **Do not waste time** on the following:

(a) an extra question–you will get no marks for it;
(b) worrying about how much anyone else is writing, they can't help you!
(c) relaxing at the end with time to spare–you do not have any. Work up to the very moment the invigilator tells you to stop writing. Check and recheck your work, including spelling and punctuation. Every single mark you gain helps, and that last mark might tip the balance between success and failure–the line has to be drawn somewhere.

8 **Help the examiner.**

(a) Do not use red or green pen or pencil on your paper. Examiners usually annotate your script in red and green, and if you use the same colours it will cause unnecessary confusion.
(b) Leave some space between each answer or section of an answer. This could also help you if you remember something you wish to add to your answer when you are checking it.
(c) Number your answers as instructed. If it is question 3 you are doing, do not label it 'C'.
(d) Write neatly. It will help you to communicate effectively with the examiner who is trying to read your script.

# Glossary of literary terms

Mere knowledge of the words in this list or other specialist words used when studying literature is not sufficient. You must know when to use a particular term, and be able to describe what it contributes to that part of the work which is being discussed.

For example, merely to label something as being a metaphor does not help an examiner or teacher to assess your response to the work being studied. You must go on to analyse what the literary device contributes to the work. Why did the author use a metaphor at all? Why not some other literary device? What extra sense of feeling or meaning does the metaphor convey to the reader? How effective is it in supporting the author's intention? What was the author's intention, as far as you can judge, in using that metaphor?

Whenever you use a particular literary term you must do so with a purpose and that purpose usually involves an explanation and expansion upon its use. Occasionally you will simply use a literary term 'in passing', as, for example, when you refer to the 'narrator' of a story as opposed to the 'author'–they are not always the same! So please be sure that you understand both the meaning and purpose of each literary term you employ.

This list includes only those words which we feel will assist in helping you to understand the major concepts in play and novel construction. It makes no attempt to be comprehensive. These are the concepts which examiners frequently comment upon as being inadequately grasped by many students. Your teacher will no doubt expand upon this list and introduce you to other literary devices and words within the context of the particular work/s you are studying–the most useful place to experience and explore them and their uses.

**Plot** This is the plan or story of a play or novel. Just as a body has a skeleton to hold it together, so the plot forms the 'bare bones' of the work of literature in play or novel form. It is however, much more than this. It is arranged in time, so one of the things which encourages us to continue reading is to see what happens next. It deals with causality, that is how one event or incident causes another. It has a sequence, so that in general, we move from the beginning through to the end.

**Structure** The arrangement and interrelationship of parts in a play or novel are obviously bound up with the plot. An examination of how the author has structured his work will lead us to consider the function of, say, the 43 letters which are such an important part of *Pride and Prejudice*. We would consider the arrangement of the time-sequence in *Wuthering Heights* with its 'flashbacks' and their association with the different narrators of the story. In a play we would look at the scene divisions and how different events are placed in a relationship so as to produce a particular effect; where soliloquies occur so as to inform the audience of a character's innermost emotions and feelings. Do be aware that great works of fiction are not just simply thrown together by their authors. We study a work in detail, admiring its parts and the intricacies of its structure. The reason for a work's greatness has to do with the genius of its author and the care of its construction. Ultimately, though, we do well to remember that it is the work as a whole that we have to judge, not just the parts which make up that whole.

*Glossary of literary terms*

**Narrator** A narrator tells or relates a story. In *Wuthering Heights* various characters take on the task of narrating the events of the story: Cathy, Heathcliff, etc, as well as being, at other times, central characters taking their part in the story. Sometimes the author will be there, as it were, in person, relating and explaining events. The method adopted in telling the story relates very closely to style and structure.

**Style** The manner in which something is expressed or performed, considered as separate from its intrinsic content or meaning. It might well be that a lyrical, almost poetical style will be used, for example concentrating on the beauties and contrasts of the natural world as a foil to the narration of the story and creating emotions in the reader which serve to heighten reactions to the events being played out on the page. It might be that the author uses a terse, almost staccato approach to the conveyance of his story. There is no simple route to grasping the variations of style which are to be found between different authors or indeed within one novel. The surest way to appreciate this difference is to read widely and thoughtfully and to analyse and appreciate the various strategies which an author uses to command our attention.

**Character** A person represented in a play or story. However, the word also refers to the combination of traits and qualities distinguishing the individual nature of a person or thing. Thus, a characteristic is one such distinguishing quality: in *Pride and Prejudice*, the pride and prejudices of various characters are central to the novel, and these characteristics which are associated with Mr Darcy, Elizabeth, and Lady Catherine in that novel, enable us to begin assessing how a character is reacting to the surrounding events and people. Equally, the lack of a particular trait or characteristic can also tell us much about a character.

**Character development** In *Pride and Prejudice*, the extent to which Darcy's pride, or Elizabeth's prejudice is altered, the recognition by those characters of such change, and the events of the novel which bring about the changes are central to any exploration of how a character develops, for better or worse.

**Irony** This is normally taken to be the humorous or mildly sarcastic use of words to imply the opposite of what they say. It also refers to situations and events and thus you will come across references such as prophetic, tragic, and dramatic irony.

**Dramatic irony** This occurs when the implications of a situation or speech are understood by the audience but not by all or some of the characters in the play or novel. We also class as ironic words spoken innocently but which a later event proves either to have been mistaken or to have prophesied that event. When we read in the play *Macbeth*:

> *Macbeth*
> Tonight we hold a solemn supper, sir,
> And I'll request your presence.
>
> *Banquo*
> Let your highness
> Command upon me, to the which my duties
> Are with a most indissoluble tie
> Forever knit.

we, as the audience, will shortly have revealed to us the irony of Macbeth's words. He does not expect Banquo to attend the supper as he plans to have Banquo murdered before the supper occurs. However, what Macbeth does not know is the prophetic irony of Banquo's response. His 'duties. . . a most indissoluble tie' will be fulfilled by his appearance at the supper as a ghost–something Macbeth certainly did not forsee or welcome, and which Banquo most certainly did not have in mind!

**Tragedy** This is usually applied to a play in which the main character, usually a person of importance and outstanding personal qualities, falls to disaster through the combination of personal failing and circumstances with which he cannot deal. Such tragic happenings may also be central to a novel. In *The Mayor of Casterbridge*, flaws in Henchard's character are partly responsible for his downfall and eventual death.

In Shakespeare's plays, *Macbeth* and *Othello*, the tragic heroes from which the two plays take their names, are both highly respected and honoured men who have proven their outstanding personal qualities. Macbeth, driven on by his ambition and that of his very determined wife, kills his king. It leads to civil war in his country, to his own eventual downfall and death, and to his wife's suicide. Othello, driven to an insane jealousy by the cunning of his lieutenant, Iago, murders his own innocent wife and commits suicide.

**Satire** Where topical issues, folly or evil are held up to scorn by means of ridicule and irony–the satire may be subtle or openly abusive.

In *Animal Farm*, George Orwell used the rebellion of the animals against their oppressive owner to satirize the excesses of the Russian revolution at the beginning of the 20th century. It would be a mistake, however, to see the satire as applicable only to that event. There is a much wider application of that satire to political and social happenings both before and since the Russian revolution and in all parts of the world.

**Images** An image is a mental representation or picture. One that constantly recurs in *Macbeth* is clothing, sometimes through double meanings of words: 'he seems rapt withal', 'Why do you dress me in borrowed robes?', 'look how our partner's rapt', 'Like our strange garments, cleave not to their mould', 'Whiles I stood rapt in the wonder of it', 'which would be worn now in their newest gloss', 'Was the hope drunk Wherein you dressed yourself?', 'Lest our old robes sit easier than our new.', 'like a giant's robe upon a dwarfish thief'. All these images serve to highlight and comment upon aspects of Macbeth's behaviour and character. In Act 5, Macbeth the loyal soldier who was so honoured by his king at the start of the play, struggles to regain some small shred of his self-respect. Three times he calls to Seyton for his armour, and finally moves toward his destiny with the words 'Blow wind, come wrack, At least we'll die with harness on our back'–his own armour, not the borrowed robes of a king he murdered.

Do remember that knowing a list of images is not sufficient. You must be able to interpret them and comment upon the contribution they make to the story being told.

**Theme** A unifying idea, image or motif, repeated or developed throughout a work.

In *Pride and Prejudice*, a major theme is marriage. During the course of the novel we are shown various views of and attitudes towards marriage. We actually witness the relationships of four different couples through their courtship, engagement and eventual marriage. Through those events and the examples presented to us in the novel of other already married couples, the author engages in a thorough exploration of the theme.

This list is necessarily short. There are whole books devoted to the explanation of literary terms. Some concepts, like style, need to be experienced and discussed in a group setting with plenty of examples in front of you. Others, such as dramatic irony, need keen observation from the student and a close knowledge of the text to appreciate their significance and existence. All such specialist terms are well worth knowing. But they should be used only if they enable you to more effectively express your knowledge and appreciation of the work being studied.

## Titles in the series

### A level
Coriolanus
The Pardoner's Tale

### GCSE
Animal Farm
The Crucible
Far from the Madding Crowd
Great Expectations
Hobson's Choice
An Inspector Calls
Jane Eyre
Lord of the Flies
Macbeth
A Man for All Seasons
The Mayor of Casterbridge
A Midsummer Night's Dream
Of Mice and Men
Pride and Prejudice
Pygmalion
Romeo and Juliet
To Kill A Mockingbird
Wuthering Heights